Employing
Linguistics

ALSO AVAILABLE FROM BLOOMSBURY

Employing Linguistics

Thinking and Talking about Careers for Linguists

ANNA MARIE TRESTER

BLOOMSBURY ACADEMIC
LONDON • NEW YORK • OXFORD • NEW DELHI • SYDNEY

BLOOMSBURY ACADEMIC
Bloomsbury Publishing Plc
50 Bedford Square, London, WC1B 3DP, UK
1385 Broadway, New York, NY 10018, USA
29 Earlsfort Terrace, Dublin 2, Ireland

BLOOMSBURY, BLOOMSBURY ACADEMIC and the Diana logo are trademarks
of Bloomsbury Publishing Plc

First published in Great Britain 2022

Cover design by Rebecca Heselton

Bloomsbury Publishing Plc does not have any control over, or responsibility for,
any third-party websites referred to or in this book. All internet addresses given
in this book were correct at the time of going to press. The author and publisher
regret any inconvenience caused if addresses have changed or sites have ceased
to exist, but can accept no responsibility for any such changes.

A catalogue record for this book is available from the British Library.

Library of Congress Cataloging-in-Publication Data
Names: Trester, Anna Marie, author.
Title: Employing linguistics : thinking and talking about careers for linguists /
Anna Marie Trester.
Description: London ; New York : Bloomsbury Academic, 2022. |
Includes bibliographical references and index. |
Identifiers: LCCN 2021037591 (print) | LCCN 2021037592 (ebook) |
ISBN 9781350137950 (hardback) | ISBN 9781350137967 (paperback) |
ISBN 9781350137981 (pdf) | ISBN 9781350137974 (ebook)
Subjects: LCSH: Linguistics–Vocational guidance. |
Linguists. Classification: LCC P60 .T74 2022 (print) | LCC P60 (ebook) |
DDC 410.23–dc23/eng/20211105
LC record available at https://lccn.loc.gov/2021037591
LC ebook record available at https://lccn.loc.gov/2021037592

ISBN: HB: 978-1-3501-3795-0
PB: 978-1-3501-3796-7
ePDF: 978-1-3501-3798-1
eBook: 978-1-3501-3797-4

Typeset by Newgen KnowledgeWorks Pvt. Ltd., Chennai, India
Printed and bound in Great Britain

To find out more about our authors and books visit www.bloomsbury.com
and sign up for our newsletters.

Contents

Figures

Preface: From Nebulous to Nebulae

Stories are tools for noticing.
They help us notice.

The stories that we hear shape our sense of who we are and what we can do.

First and foremost, this book has been created to share stories. Linguists need to hear different—and different kinds of—career stories. We need to hear about a broad range—a constellation!—of contexts in which our skills and training may be employed. And crucially, we need to hear more of them in the midst of their unfolding.

As I look around at the multifaceted and complex challenges facing our world, I see both limitless potential and great need for the ways linguists think, including an empirical orientation to change, the ability to look below apparent chaos to reveal patterns, and the ability to see and think in systems. When our community has a better picture of the breadth of purposes and problems to which our linguistic skills and training may be put—and gets a better sense for the universe of possibilities—we will feel our value and dream big about our futures.

We will also come to recognize that feelings of uncertainty and disorientation are not only normal, but to be expected when sparking new connections.

In my own case, I came to this sense of abundance experientially. I had the opportunity to learn about a breadth and range of possibilities over the course of running a professionally oriented sociolinguistic MA program for more than six years. I learned alongside and from my students, and you will hear many of their stories over the course of this book—especially in Chapter 2—where I share the stories of ten students, ten years after their graduation.

I am so grateful to the founder of that program, Dr. Deborah Schiffrin, who encouraged me to apply for the director job, when I was thinking instead only of jobs on the tenure track. I couldn't see it at the time, but her perspective and experience uniquely enabled her to see what I brought to the position from my previous work experience in the financial sector, in broadcast journalism, and the nonprofit and arts sectors. When I was first hired, she gave me as my first assignment the task of conducting fifty informational interviews that first semester. Informational interviews—conversations with people about the day-to-day of their work—would give me the context that I needed to be able to show students the breadth and range of their professional possibilities.

I'm certain that I did not make the target of 50 informational interviews. What did happen, however, was that I sat down and thought about everyone I knew or wanted to know (former colleagues, linguistics department alum, my former and current classmates, prospective students) and think about what questions I might like to pose to them about their work. As I now know, one of the most important things about an informational interview is that it places you in a learning mindset, a growth mindset. It is itself an ask. It involves making yourself slightly vulnerable to tell someone that you need something from them. And when you engage with people in this way, you build community and create opportunities. One of my first interviews was with an old boss at MacNeill Lehrer who offered me an opportunity to do some consulting. One linguist who I spoke with knew she was very happy in her professional life, but she wanted to hear from me, from the fifty others I had talked to—did she seem to be the happiest?

I hope this book inspires you to get out there and start asking for stories. And I hope you get to speak to many of the happiest linguists. Listen to the stories for what ideas they spark for you. Because this will build our community. This will create opportunity. Because the world needs linguists.

Acknowledgments

First of all, I need to thank from the very bottom of my heart, all of the generous people who shared their professional experiences with me. Without you, this book would not exist. I appreciate your trust in me to tell the stories the way that I wanted them to be told and your wisdom to push back when necessary. And whether or not your story appears in the final (greatly edited-down) version or not, you shaped this book, and I am humbled to have been entrusted with the gifts of your stories!

To Katie Nelson for herding all of the cats. I would not have made it through the race much less across the finish line without your clear-headed sagacity.

To Criscillia Benford for deep listening that held the entirety of this arc long enough to help me see the structure and make the signposts.

To Carole Sargent for helping me face my deepest fears and realizing that I am just a hell of a lot stronger than all that noise!

To Erica, for making my California Adventure possible in the first place.

Annette Simmons for helping me see that "it's not about where you've been, it's about where you're going" is a collaborative narrative.

Trudy Hale and my writing family at the Porches.

Heidi and John for being my family—you know what you did, and I love you for it!

Kirsten for taking walks with me and asking me lots of thought-provoking WHYs along the way.

Sincere gratitude to Aaron Dolina, Yesha Malla, and Chelsea McCracken for close reading and feedback on drafts.

And finally, to the team at Bloomsbury Academic for believing in the project, letting me have my voice, giving me the title I wanted, and creating cover art that celebrates the adventure—thank you for "getting it." ☺

Introduction: Charting the Stars

In *Bringing Linguistics to Work* (BLx2W), I shared a handful of stories about linguists and their career paths using the metaphor of journey—and its metaphorical entailments—to explore the twists and turns of navigating a career. The storytelling focused on decision points: the moments when each linguist made a decision to take a different path.

In a way, the creation of that book ended up being a signpost for me as well. Upon its completion, I decided to head off in an entirely different professional direction. I quit my full-time job, moved to California, and immersed myself in the world of applied storytelling, meeting many folks who engage in this work, including Laura Packer, Thayler Pekar, Annette Simmons, and Victoria Ward. I also met my business partner Criscillia Benford, and Shawn Callahan of Anecdote International, with whom Criscillia and I have had the opportunity to apprentice for the past couple years. This has been a very invigorating time, but it has also been a very confusing one as well. I had no clear path forward, and I seemed to be learning more about what I didn't want to do than what I did.

And now, at the time of writing, we are embarking on a collective time of radical change and societal transformation. As I write in the spring of 2021, it feels like everything has rapidly shifted, including—and perhaps especially—the world of work.

From my own experience of productive disorientation, I found a metaphor to help me that I hope will be helpful for readers in navigating these times of rapid change. This is the metaphor of charting the stars. If we think about the present moment through this concept, we might say that our entire cosmology has shifted. We can no longer take for granted so many things that we did before. We need to find our bearings again. This will come from finding our north stars, the things that we can use to hold firm as we navigate the uncertainty, ambiguity, and rapid change.

I began *Bringing Linguistics to Work* with a story about a walk in the desert with my cousin Kirsten, which I found to be a helpful illustration of the journey metaphor. As it happens, I now live in the desert southwest, and it was again on a walk with this same cousin that I found a little nugget that might illuminate the energy source of the storytelling in this book: stories and stars.

I took Kirsten to go walk on a labyrinth just after sunset in the mountains near her house. This particular labyrinth is nestled on the west-facing side of a hill with a panoramic view of the city of Tucson with lots and lots of sky. Although the sun had set about twenty minutes before, it wasn't fully dark yet, and we were starting to be able to see the stars but we still had enough of a glow from the west to see our steps.

Walking a labyrinth wasn't something we had done together before, so she was curious about why—what it meant to me. I love labyrinths, but no one had asked me "why" before, and I realized it is concurrent with my own recent and more regular practice of meditation. Kirsten had recently been to China, and visited many Buddhist temples, so she was curious about the kind of meditation I do and its relationship to Buddhism. She's a very good listener and she asks great questions, and as we talked and I shared stories and the stars became brighter, I realized that it had been a while since I had taken stock of where I was, where I had been, and where I was going. I hadn't really thought much about my spiritual practice recently—particularly with all the chaos of the past sixteen months of the pandemic. But the conversation was giving me perspective. The more consistent practice that I had been doing during the pandemic had solidified some things that I hadn't realized.

Kirsten and I were both raised Catholic, but I have been on something of a spiritual quest for most of my adult life. While she still worships at a Catholic church (where there is also a beautiful labyrinth, I hasten to add), I have been a seeker in many Christian traditions, Episcopalian, Methodist, and Unitarian, and for most of the early 2000s attended Quaker meetings. I started learning more about Buddhism about four years ago, but really settled into a regular practice only in the last year. And, while Catholicism to Buddhism may seem like a big leap, I didn't experience the moves that way— they felt like a slow, steady, natural progression—especially from Quakerism to Buddhism.

But as I was telling Kirsten, I realized that it was only just recently that I could even make sense of the progression. The process was confusing and disorienting as it was unfolding. And, at many points along the way, people felt the need to tell me how strange my choices were and just how different these practices were to one another. With hindsight, I see that those people probably just didn't know enough of one or another tradition to make that assessment, or just didn't see things the way I saw them. Which is of course fine—it all makes sense to me now. But it would have been great to hear the same from someone at the time who could see how it all made sense. I was following my intuition and practicing and learning as I went, and finding what worked and what didn't, but I couldn't really see how things connected (especially how where I had been connected with where I currently was), and I certainly didn't know where I was heading (and I still don't know where I will end up)!

At this point in our conversation, the stars were shining brightly and we could start looking for constellations. Kirsten has this app that requires you to hold your phone up to the sky and it maps the stars into constellations. It even works during the day, revealing what is there but hard to see!

So here's the parallel to the stories I share in this book.

At any moment, as you are experiencing your own story, there are opportunities to recognize patterns, but in many cases, you can't see the whole picture yet, you might only have a bright spot or two. You can't recognize and understand those until there are other bright spots to put it in context. But the practice of finding those bright spots is the way forward. I'm picturing you as you read this book, remembering, and identifying more of your own bright sparks and northern stars: organizations or people whose work really sparks your interest; a project where you lit up while you were working on it; some theoretical framework that energizes you; or an electric conversation that you had recently. I'm hoping that the storytelling helps you draw connections to possible sources of that spark, other expressions of that spark, potential future applications of that spark.

In each of the stories I share, I bring focus on a bright spot—one idea or one moment from this person's experience that grabs my attention. In pulling forward these bright spots—these sparks—one single aspect of their work that exemplifies a linguist's way of thinking in action, I draw a link to something I see about a linguist's way of thinking, doing, seeing. Not every one of these sparks will speak to you, and you probably wouldn't draw the same connections I do, but I am hoping at least a handful of them spark with you in ways that help you gain perspective and insight that help you navigate your own night sky.

Ideally, you will generate many sparks, around which you will build stories (using the STAR method, described later in the book), resulting ideally in a hundred or more. This collection of bright spots will give you enough raw material to begin cataloging, charting them into constellations.

Constellations point toward connection and meaning found in patterns. And here is an important thing to know about the storytelling in this book: It is in the collection of these stories that patterns start to emerge. I want to ask you to read the stories in this way: making sense of them as parts of a system. Some of these linguists were trained as semanticists, some as phonologists, many as sociolinguists—and because I am a sociolinguist, my network is rather socio-heavy—and indeed, the book is focused on the US context. You will even see that it is tilted slightly toward the western part of the Unites States where I spent the majority of my time as I developed the book over the course of the past four years. But the mindset that I want to invite you to adopt as you read their stories is one of curious reflection: Which bright spots spark your imagination? What do they illuminate as a congregate? Do you see any commonalities with your own interests and ways of thinking? Differences are very useful to note as well.

Stars connect us to the domain of energy, of fuel, prompting the questions: What is energizing for you? What has been before? Where do you sense that might be in the future? Paying attention to your energy is one of your north stars. Some stars are highly explosive, and then they burn out—you might have already experienced this phenomenon and are aiming for experiences that are more sustainable for the long term. Given that each of us only has so much time and energy, how do you want to spend yours?

During a recent workshop, a participant told me that when it came to thinking about career, she was "lost in the woods." I invited her to imagine that she could look up. The domain of careers is expansive, largely uncharted, but navigable. And there are many tools that can help us navigate.

For me, one of those tools is story itself.

Story was one of the main reasons I moved to the Bay Area in 2016. I had heard in countless conversations that the Bay Area was the place to be for someone interested in (business) applications of story. My thinking about story has evolved over the course of these past few years, shaped by myriad conversations with those engaged in story work, resulting in a focus on story listening (more than story telling), and an accompanying shift to focus more on story function than on story structure. Certainly, this is owing to overexposure to one particular form—that of the hero's journey—overly subscribed to in business circles. There are so many other forms and so many other ways that stories can have an impact on those who listen to them.

I seek to tell stories that inspire and motivate curiosity. I hope to nudge readers to find more (and different kinds of) stories about work, and I hope you will listen to them differently and begin telling them differently.

Stories can serve many *functions*—in this case, I especially hope to expand noticing. But I also hope they inspire, challenge, and teach. They can also serve to normalize things like uncertainty—which is why I especially sought stories about charting previously uncharted territories, and stories in the midst of their unfolding—as I have done with linguists Samantha Beaver, Didem Ikizoğlu, Esther Surenthiraraj, and Jeremy Rud who were generous to share their active early career navigation with readers of this book.

Career stories shared by or with former academics often begin with the "decision" to leave "academia"—and this is how they often get framed by the questioner. Or they start way back with the moment that this storyteller has identified in hindsight as the place where it all began. Instead, I begin with the now. And I invite thinking about what comes next. Because we are all in the midst of an unfolding story. Because when it comes to career, it's not so much about where you have been, but where you are heading.

About the Stories in This Book

The stories in this book are constructed to bring focus to what a particular linguist does now.

And in the here and now, I identify some specific aspect of language (adjacency pairs in Greg Bennet's story in Chapter 3) or conceptual framework (like identity theory in Chapter 5) to suggest at the broader need for our uniquely honed powers of analysis and observation. I do not argue that any of us will use all of the skills in a linguist's skillset in any context. Rather, I hope to show that the myriad skills we possess might (already) be (being) employed in contexts beyond what has been proscribed to us. I suggest that when we think broadly about how our skills can be more widely employed, we get back in touch with what energizes us, and what it means to be a linguist in the world, which gives us the energy we need to tackle the significant challenges that exist in our world.

You may notice that some of these stories are quite short, some of them just a few sentences. This enables me to build a wider constellation, include more stories—nearly forty of them!—drawn from varied worlds of work and from a wide geographical scope. Additionally, this choice to tell shorter stories helps to reinforce the telescoping in on moments. We need to pay attention to moments of everyday experience because career—like life—is experienced in moments. And it is by paying attention to these moments that you might just catch the flash of a spark. In this immediacy of the "here and how" I hope you can connect to your own energy, momentum, and agency to practice noticing sparks, drawing links, and making connections.

Since 2017, I have been teaching a five-week course that I call Career Camp, where participants gather every week around a virtual campfire (on the teleconferencing platform Zoom) and share stories. One of the most powerful aspects of this experience is the perspective that you gain once you have heard a handful of stories from your other participants. As a story listener, you start to be able to clearly see patterns in the way that each person works. And they can see patterns in your stories.

Recently, one camper named Bill dazzled the group with his ability to innovate creative solutions to seemingly intractable problems, as exemplified in a story that he told about a moment when he needed to improvise and innovate as a sound technician. See what this story helps you notice about his adaptability, creativity, and problem-solving.

My tech expertise is in the areas of audio, video, or computers. My favorite problem-solving story comes from a video production I was once on. The room we were given to film in had a horrifically loud air conditioning noise in it, and this was back in the days before we had audio cleanup plugins on our computers. I said, "We have to get that AC turned off if we're going to film in this room." There were no other rooms available, and the AC could not be shut off because it would shut it off for the entire building. The producer looked at me and said, "What are we going to do? What can we do? ... Short of cancelling the shoot ... " I thought long and hard, and suddenly had an idea. What if I can trick the thermostat in the room into thinking it's cooler than it is. So I gaffer taped 2 cold cans of soda over the top of the thermostat. And sure enough, a minute later, the AC shut off, and we were able to have a successful shoot. I'm exactly the type of person you want to have around when you run into challenges/problems. It can mean the difference between meeting expectations and delivering or failing and having to cancel your shoot.

Bill's not a linguist, but the degree to which he values clarity of communication is on full display here in this story. You notice that he will go above and beyond to ensure the best context for a clear recording, and you know that Bill really cares about his work without him having to say so.

Ironically, many of us don't even recognize our own sparks because they have become such an integral part of how we work. And for those of us who have been in school a long time, surrounded by linguists, we forget that not everyone is trained to think like us. Also, that we won't always be one of many linguists, and indeed we have unique interests, ways of combining and employing the same skills and training, even among our peers.

I have structured this book with the aim of simulating the experience of close story listening in a group for you as a reader.

By bringing together a bunch of stories, I hope to enable you to see some of the things that make you unique, and also feel how powerfully we can impact the world together. Some major themes that emerge from the book help us know how to make this happen including becoming more comfortable with discomfort, navigating ambiguity, recognizing productive disorientation, being ok with not knowing, and cultivating flexibility and adaptability because we are always operating in contexts of change.

Speaking of "we," bringing people together, and having broader impact—a word now about who this book is for.

If You Are Interested in a Linguistic Approach to Career, This Book Is for You

In 2011, I was standing on the Mars simulator at the NASA Ames Research Center in Palo Alto, California, with Charlotte Linde. We were having a conversation about linguists at work. She worked at NASA at the time, and I couldn't yet appreciate how the interplanetary conceptual frame for this book was beginning to take shape, but she made an offhand observation that I probably knew more about careers for linguists than just about anyone at that moment, which made me realize that I had been spending too much of my time and energy worried about the handful of people who seemed to be disapproving of how publicly I had been thinking and talking about professional applications of our skills.

As a PhD student, I had gotten wrapped up in the narrative that there is only one acceptable career path—that of the tenured academic, and at that point in 2011, after four years of being on the academic job market, I decided to close that door. And there were so many loud voices clamoring for my attention about what that meant. There are many who would story that as a personal failing and want to say there is not a place for career education in academia, stemming from the misplaced notion that somehow it takes something away from the integrity and rigor of our discipline to think about how it might be made accessible, shared, and more widely applied or "employed." Charlotte's comment (and indeed the evident impact and palpable joy she derives from her work) reminded me that I don't believe application takes away any of the rigor, that in fact, I think application is additive. I decided to stop participating in conversations about who gets to call themselves a linguist, and decided that what I am interested in is what you do, not who you are (or who wants to tell you who you are not).

I decided to take things up a notch.

With Anastasia Nylund (whose story you will hear in Chapter 6), we re-instated the Linguistics Beyond Academia Special Interest Group at the Linguistics Society of America. I reached out to Dave Sayers, who at the time was creating the Ling-Outside listserv in the UK, and we collaborated on events and activities like resume and LinkedIn workshops. It was at one of the LinkedIn workshops where I met Nancy Frishberg, who maintains a group in the Bay Area called Bay CHI (Computer–Human Interaction, where I met Janneke, who we will meet in Chapter 3). I started working on *Bringing Linguistics to Work*, and I started my blog which has introduced me to many hundreds of people and led to the formation of an online community that I now run called the CL Mighty Network.

And I am now having a broader, more expansive conversation about careers for linguists with like-minded folks who believe that the world of work needs linguists and that such an arrangement where we bring linguistics to work can be mutually beneficial.

Take the last month as an example (at the time of writing this chapter in January 2021). It is the beginning of the year, a time when many people become reflective about their lives, including career. I have been reached out to by students in high school looking for career information to help them decide whether or not they want to study linguistics in college. I have been contacted by students studying linguistics at the college, graduate, and doctoral levels. Faculty reach out to me, as do researchers investigating the career outcomes of linguistics students. I have talked to folks who have been graduated for two months and folks who have been out for two decades. They want to talk about things like getting a job, changing jobs, changing the job they currently have (job crafting, more on that soon). And I don't just hear from linguists. In this past month, I have talked to an economist, a sociologist, a geographer, and an actor. I'm happy to talk about career with anyone who is interested in a linguist's take, a story approach.

All of which is to say that:

If you are a current student of linguistics, starting to envision your future, this book is for you.

If you are a professor, looking to gather information for your students (or for yourself), this book is for you.

If you once read a book about linguistics twenty years ago, and are curious about how linguistic thinking might inform your thinking about how you work, this book is for you.

I simply ask that you bring curiosity, a spirit of exploration and adventure, and linguistically honed listening skills. Come on in, let's check out some possibilities, look for yourself and ask, "What's here for me?"

Notice.

Because with awareness, comes choice.

Here's Our Plan

I call Chapter 1 "Reckoning with Your Intentions" and I use it to tell the story of three women whose stories powerfully invite us to think about why and how we employ linguistics. I focus on three linguists at various stages of their careers: someone embarking on a new research enterprise in retirement, someone at the very beginning of the process of launching a business, and someone at the vanguard, leading a hugely important transformation of our field. We'll reckon with erasure, white supremacy, and our field's history of racism. To conclude the chapter, spurred by the idea of sparking connection, I share a connection story from my own professional experience and give a catalyst for readers—as I will do at the end of each chapter.

In Chapter 2, "BRIGHTEN While You Work," I share stories from ten former students, ten years after graduating with their MA in linguistics.

Over the years, as these ten have changed jobs, gotten promoted, gotten married and had children, moved, moved back, and so on, their experiences illuminate some broad patterns about work, including the range of contexts in which our skills and training may be applied. I share their experiences using the acronym BRIGHTEN: Business, Research, Innovation, Government, Healthcare Communication, Technology, Education, and Nonprofit. It is my hope that over the course of listening to their work stories, and as you see them move back and forth across some of the perceived barriers or central dualities—in so doing, revealing them to be false dichotomies—this will expand not only your understanding of the contexts and the domains in which we linguists can operate, but also that you will gain a sense of greater professional agency. Agency is something we will explore through the idea catalyst of jobcrafting at the end of the chapter.

In Chapter 3, "HOW Linguists BRIGHTEN," I focus in on one world of work from the BRIGHTEN acronym—Research (R)—and more specifically User Experience (UX) Research, a field that has witnessed a tremendous boom as I have been researching and writing this book. To introduce the reader to the world of UX, I get a bit "meta" and do user research with a linguist herself learning about this world of work. Finding clues in what she notices in a research portfolio, I draw links to the things prospective employers might ask of job candidates. We then turn to the stories of user researchers (and their colleagues) who illuminate the ways that thinking and working like a linguist is helpful in this world of work.

I call Chapter 4 "Decide to BRIGHTEN Here and Now" because it shows what it means to pay attention for opportunities to employ linguistics in the "here and now." Drawing inspiration from a creative campaign where the idea of being lost is an invitation to be present to the now/here, I remind readers how we might benefit from broadening the timescales of our thinking and understanding our experience of now in a much wider social and temporal context. I share stories from linguists at the doctor's office, reflecting on organizational norms and practices, and even commuting on the bus. Their stories invite us to pay attention like linguists to the here and now of this historical moment in the places we live and work and travel. The activities at the end are a set of practices for being present to the affordances of the moment.

Chapter 5, "BRIGHTEN Around the World," moves us from the "here and how" to consider something of the "there and then" by listening to stories from around the world. These help us to ultimately realize not only how very interconnected we all are, but also how we can begin to think about our shared future as a planet. We'll hear from linguists working in artificial intelligence (AI), e-commerce, and even Twitter. We'll even hear from a former professor about how the process of making business more sustainable is like the process of getting a PhD. We'll conclude by hearing about language activism and cultural heritage, considering how and why we can look for ways to use linguistic theory and language awareness to broaden our understanding of identity and be more inclusive. The story catalyst at the end of the chapter will invite readers into a reflection about the impact of their work.

In the last content chapter, "Navigate Your Career with WHY," we play with a theme of interrogating our work through a collection of stories focused on the WHY of our work (which includes our lives outside the workplace). We'll start with a story about librarianship (and five WHYs behind that WHY). From there, we'll move to an entrepreneur, whose WHY has become being able to provide work opportunities for other linguists. We'll talk to a copy writer who shares a bit of the satisfaction he derives from being able to find "useful words," and from someone whose work with the CIA has enabled her to be there at critical moments when a deeper awareness of language was necessary. Finally, we'll think about the role of language and story in changing the global conversation about issues like income inequality, the increasing uncomfortability of capitalism, and climate change.

Note: Some of the linguists who shared their stories were unable to give names (theirs or that of their company) for various reasons. When you see only a first name, that might be a pseudonym, and when you see no name at all, that was the linguist's choice for presentation of their story.

I hope these stories, activities, and themes spark ideas and catalyze momentum for you as you chart your own constellations and find uncharted galaxies.

1

Reckoning with Your Intentions

I invoke the idea of "reckoning" in this chapter because the stories comprising it showcase three powerful linguists in career-defining moments, moments where they take decisive action to show what they are made of. These stories show what they stand for and how they think and work like linguists. And note an important distinction that I draw here, one that I maintain throughout the book. I contend that once you have been trained in our ways of seeing, your linguistics training shapes how you frame problems and how you approach your work, such that you work *like* a linguist, even if you are not working *as* a linguist. I choose to focus on what the linguist DOES rather than whether or not this person IS a linguist (a line of inquiry that I have found to be counterproductive in discussions about career).

By focusing in on a moment from their professional lives, I hope to invite you—the reader—to reflect a bit on some of the moments (career-defining or ordinary), which showcase how you work like a linguist, whether or not you are currently working *as* one.

We'll begin with Charlotte Linde, focusing in on the moment when NASA Ames reached out to ask: "Do you think you might have something to say about small group decision-making in the cockpit?" A moment where she felt the fear and did it anyway.

Charlotte's career encompasses more than thirty years of wide-ranging career adventure and a breadth of applications from ethnographies with insurance agencies, Silicon Valley, and Buddhist communities, to multiple engagements with NASA, including her now famous research on pilot and air-traffic-controller communication. Her engagement with both academic and applied research in many domains of work exemplifies important career lessons for those at any stage of their career journey. As Charlotte put it: "Go out there and do stuff. One thing will lead to another."

In telling her story, I seek to inspire those of you considering what it might mean to say "yes" to an opportunity that might be in front of you at present, or to one that you are thinking about creating. Or perhaps you are in a period of reflection, and you might want to think about those to which you have said "yes" or "no" in the past in terms of how they have shaped your trajectory, and whether you might currently be in a moment of reorientation. As you listen to Charlotte's story, think about your own whys, including why you do what you do, and why you do things the way you do them.

Charlotte Linde

"Go Out and Do Stuff, One Thing Will Lead to Another"

When she got that first call from NASA, Charlotte had no experience with communication in the cockpit. And the stakes were so high! But she trusted her training, and she trusted that the research process would illuminate useful insights and she said "yes." I have long been inspired by Charlotte's careful, thoughtful, and densely intricate work, dating back I suppose to my first reading her book *Life Stories* as a graduate student. I reached out back then with a note thanking her for this excellent work, describing how it was helping me with some project that I was working on. That began a conversation that has continued for years, and now, Charlotte presents me with an opportunity to take her advice—to go for it. Despite feeling a bit intimidated, I'll take a whack at telling her powerful career story because I trust the process that I have developed for the storytelling in this book, starting (if unconventionally) with the here and now.

Charlotte is currently doing research focused on exemplars—people who get held up by communities as examples for how to be—as part of a larger project exploring the social construction of wisdom in various organizations. This research draws from three of her own long-term projects: (1) an ethnography with a major American insurance company, as described in her book *Working the Past*; (2) a Buddhist meditation community where she has been practicing and teaching meditation for forty-plus years; and (3) Silicon Valley, drawing from her many years of living and working in this region including thirteen years as an entrepreneur. Having recently put up all her publications (going back to 1975) on ResearchGate, she is looking to invite conversational partners to explore these concepts, as happened recently when a professor at a Lutheran seminary reached out to ask if she would be willing to come talk at an annual meeting of their current students and alumni. He had read *Working the Past* and saw the connections to narrative and institutional remembering, and was delighted to learn of her interest in the ways that members of organizations come to be recognized as "people who get counted as wise within an institutional context."

Charlotte describes her expertise as that of understanding: "The ways in which institutions use narrative to remember their identity and history, and to induct new members into these ongoing stories." Reflecting on the experience of being the first woman to go speak to that particular seminary, she remarked that they saw many parallels and asked her great questions, which ultimately she concluded was unsurprising because as she realized, "these people are in the same business as I am!"

In her recent past, Charlotte worked in Knowledge Management at NASA—but this was in fact her second engagement with the National Aeronautics and Space Administration. The more recent stint started in 1999, and comprised completely different work and was a totally different "way in" than the first time (more on that one soon). Over the years, she participated on teams helping NASA design and build spacecraft, to develop collaborations with industry, and to manage the systems that organized information, knowledge, and learned wisdom including drafting requirements and conducting evaluations and trainings. As she describes it: "Such institutional narrations can be viewed as knowledge management in its natural habitat: hardly noticed, ubiquitous, and effective."

The title she used for her business card "Socio-Rocket Scientist" is my favorite job title ever, but it gives little sense for her responsibilities within the Information Sciences and Technology division at NASA Ames Research Center. Broadly speaking, she observed and advised about the practices by which NASA "remembers" or in other words how they "preserve and use representations of the past to guide present and future actions." When I describe her work to linguistics students, I tell them that her job was to chase down, organize, and preserve stories at the organization. As a linguist, she uniquely recognizes the wisdom these stories contain and the tremendous value of keeping this knowledge available and accessible to current and future employees.

Knowledge management strikes me as a great way to describe our potential as linguists to bring insight to any industry. Any linguist—no matter her theoretical orientation—will have been trained to abstract away from interaction to see the role of language in the production of knowledge as it is unfolding. Additionally, experience in managing and organizing insights will have been a part of any research project she conducts. This is just one example of how a linguist will work *like* a linguist in just about any context.

There's no doubt that Charlotte's breadth and depth of research experience made her highly sought-after when the opportunity presented itself for her to bring this expertise to NASA Ames in 1999. By that point, she had published widely in academic journals, she had worked as a Senior Research Scientist and Chief Narrative Officer at the Institute for Research on Learning, and she had run her own business, Semantic Structures, for thirteen years. But no doubt, those who were considering her candidacy would have also been interested to know that she had worked for NASA previously. So let's end this telling of Charlotte's career story by considering the moment in which it began.

When the first opportunity to work with NASA presented itself, Robin Lakoff—Charlotte's colleague at the University of California at Berkeley—had been contacted by the university's public relations department to ask about interesting research currently happening in linguistics. She told them, "Well, Charlotte is working on the Watergate tapes." They asked for a press release. Charlotte had to research the genre in order to create one, but she made a press release describing her work, and then had the "crazy good fortune" (her words) to have the story released not only during a relatively slow news week, but also at just about the same time that the David Frost interview with Richard Nixon was being run. She got picked up by the *San Francisco Chronicle* and her piece ran above the masthead—page one, above the fold. In other words, her work was featured very prominently in a major national publication. Someone from NASA Ames saw the piece, saw the potential for collaboration, and reached out.

When the call came, Charlotte was—as she puts it—completely terrified. The work was about communication in the cockpit and the stakes were very high. Lives are at stake in this context, and she wanted her research to be useful, but as she had never done research into interactions in the cockpit, she had absolutely no idea what she would find and thus no way of having certainty that what she was going to do for them was going to be useful. "What if I'm wrong?" she considered. The task, as she understood it in that moment, was to not be afraid of being afraid. She was already an experienced meditator at that time, and I can see the seeds of a mindfulness practice in helping her to see the fear and see through it at the same time. She found a way to trust her training and the research process, reassuring herself by reminding herself: "I'm an interesting person. They have interesting data. Probably I'll be able to come up with something interesting."

So what did the research reveal? Ultimately, the analysis came to focus on "mitigation," a linguistic feature which Linde and her research team defined as "a linguistic indication of indirectness and tentativeness in speech." The broad pattern that the data illuminated was that speech of subordinates is more mitigated than the speech of superiors, and the social arrangements of hierarchy in the cockpit would predict this. Much linguistic research has shown that people with less social power tend to (have to) make use of more indirect speech acts when speaking to those with more power. On a plane, the captain holds the authority to decide what gets noticed, including available topics. They found that in an emergency situation, "mitigation was a factor in failures of crewmembers to initiate discussion of new topics or have suggestions ratified by the captain" (Goguen, Linde, et al., 1986: 1). In other words, given a circumstance in which the crew noticed a problem that the captain did not, use of mitigation could lead to a failure to achieve recognition of crucial information by the person who had the institutional ability to respond.

When Malcolm Gladwell made this research context famous in his 2005 work *Blink,* he mentioned that the NTSB (National Transportation Safety Board) had been interested in mitigation for nearly fifteen years. For me, this "noisy not"[1] (something whose absence is so conspicuous that is forces you to ask "why?") makes me ask why the NTSB would have become interested in this linguistic feature? It's not as if that aspect of language is one that is on everyone's radar (if you'll forgive the pun). I suggest that the origins of this attention may have been shaped by the findings of Joseph Goguen, Charlotte Linde, and Miles Murphy in their 1986 piece "Crew Communication as a Factor in Aviation Accidents." So while Gladwell in 2005 describes how forward-thinking and unusual it was for researchers to think to look at culture as a factor in the cockpit, I applaud the ingenuity, but suggest that they were pointed in the right direction by the earlier breathtakingly creative groundbreaking work of Linde and her collaborators.

A couple of Charlotte's guiding themes—"Be interested and the world is interesting" and "Be a good collaborator and you will have many opportunities to collaborate"—explain her tendency to "swim in shoals." As a professional traveling through work over decades, there is tendency for people to bring their favorite collaborators along with them, and Charlotte has been no exception.

To close out our conversation, Charlotte reckons that the best thing she ever learned in college was working at the newspaper. She learned how to write fast to a deadline, and she also learned to manage volunteers. "A great deal of what I do now is manage volunteers. Anyone who has done this knows how hard it is to get people to do things." She has found that the best way to lead is to explain the meaning and broader purpose of the work. With a volunteer who is setting up a meditation studio, for example, the tasks might be to restock Kleenex, make sure there's water in the pitcher, and maybe sweep the floor. But the purpose of these tasks is to help those who are meditating be able to be more present, available, and open in the moment of coming together for a meditative session. The attention and mindfulness brought to the task of preparing the space will shape the experience of those who are about to sit in it.

Connecting with the why of our work is, of course, not just true of the relationship of volunteers with their tasks; we all want to make a difference in the world. And for many of us, one of the most important means for expressing our purpose will be through our work.

Bringing forward this theme—how we express ourselves through work—is one of the central reasons for choosing to talk about career through story, because stories are one of the very best ways for humans to make meaning of experience. In crafting a story, tellers decide what a particular experience means.

Samantha was brave enough to share the very uncomfortable, very vulnerable, but also very exciting moment when she decided to launch her business.

I met Samantha Beaver in the Fall of 2017 when I went to give my Bringing Linguistics to Work(shop) at the University of Wisconsin, Madison. She was finishing up her MA then, and we had a great initial conversation over lunch and stayed in touch. When I started to develop plans to write this book, she agreed to be interviewed by me at regular intervals as she began her entrepreneurial venture. She and I spoke via Zoom every couple months throughout 2018 and 2019.

And, just a note here on presentation. I don't present transcripts from every story—having been a storyteller for many years now, I have cultivated a process by which each story unfolds in its own way—but when I do present the words in the voice of the person sharing them, if I video or audio recorded the conversation, I use the transcription convention of interactional sociolinguists, presenting discourse by intonation unit, as I do here for Samantha's story.

Samantha Beaver

"OK, I'm Gonna Do It!"

In the spring of 2018 as she was gearing up for Memra's launch, Samantha spoke to me about how the opportunity came about. In Excerpt 1 below, Samantha narrates a networking meeting she had with a woman who runs a women's startup organization in Madison. As their conversation unfolded, this woman invited Samantha to participate in Forward Fest, and as we'll hear, Samantha's decision to take advantage of this opportunity becomes bigger than simply deciding whether or not to participate in this one event.

Example 1 "Ok, I'm gonna do it!"

27.	Samantha:	yeah, so this actually like wasn't like my original idea
28.		I- someone gave this idea to me and I just was like "ok, I'm gonna do it."
29.		the- there's an event in Madison called Forward Fest which is for entrepreneurs and like startups,
30.		and it's sort of more geared towards high tech.
31.		um companies but re- any startup or entrepreneur can do it,
32.		and it's uh sort of a big deal,
33.		it's like a whole week worth of um different events and activities,
34.		and it's all downtown,
35.		and people from the business community come and go.
36.		um like during the day.
37.		and there's networking events at night.
38.		and I met with someone,
39.		just um she's from uh- she was from a women's startup organization in Madison,
40.	Anna Marie:	awesome.
41.	Samantha:	and I was just connected to her I just knew her- who she was
42.		and I just like scheduled a meeting with her just to chat.
43.		about becoming involved in her organization.
44.		and she was the one that was like
45.		"oh well you know, if you're willing to get your proposal in before June first, you could host an event at Forward Fest as your official launch"

Samantha's response "Ok, I'm gonna do it!" demonstrates a moment of decisive action, adaptability, and risk-taking, but as she tells the story, she also grants us access to how emergent this decision was. She admits that she didn't feel ready at the time, which from my own entrepreneurial venture I can say is absolutely the way of things, despite the myth of the fearless entrepreneur—for more on this read Grant (2016).

To analyze this we'll move backward in this conversation, but forward in time to examine the narrative description of a speech event Samantha is anticipating in the future (her upcoming launch), using J. L. Austin's (1962) classic work *How to Do Things with Words*. Traditionally, Speech Act Theory tends to focus on performativity and performative verbs, language that DOES things (e.g., "I now pronounce you husband and wife") in the world. This locutionary act can accomplish an observable effect in the real world: the couple becoming married, if and only if the right felicity conditions are met (the person uttering them is ordained, neither person in the couple is already married, etc.), information which is known to the interlocutor, thus informing their intended effect.

And in Samantha's case, there will be a performative speech act in the event that she is gearing up for. She is looking ahead to an event where she will be able to utter the performative speech act, "I hereby launch Memra Language Services." But as she conceptualizes this future event, two months out, Samantha is also anticipating the need for other bits of language that she will want to be able to utter at this event because she anticipates a critical misunderstanding: that no one will know what she means when she says that she is a linguist.

At that event, she wants to be able to have examples of projects that can help potential clients understand what she does. She wants to give them "a box for linguists."

Example 2 "I wanna give 'em a box"

1.	Samantha:	well and that's the hard thing is that
2.		um. Nobody has a box for linguists
3.	Anna Marie:	No
4.	Samantha:	like you know if you say "I'm a linguist"
5.		they don't have a little box in their brain where they put you in the linguist box
6.		bec- but people like boxes and they need boxes
7.		because we're humans and that's how we [organize information]
8.	Anna Marie:	[@@@@@@]

9. Samantha:	so if I tell someone I'm a linguist they don't know what I am talking about.
10. Anna Marie:	Right
11: Samantha:	and so I have to-
12.	I knew right away that before the launch I had to have done this multiple times,
13. Anna Marie:	Right
14. Samantha:	for different types of people,
15.	have a few testimonials
16. Anna Marie:	yeah.
17. Samantha:	so that I could say "here are some examples."
18. Anna Marie:	right.
19. Samantha:	cause that's the only way they're going to develop that box and I know they need it,
20.	I wanna give 'em a box!

Samantha here demonstrates both working *as* and working *like* a linguist. On the one hand, her business is about working *as* a linguist—it involves direct application of linguistic analytical methods—but at the same time, the ways in which she is approaching her work—including how she is approaching this launch event—demonstrates a linguistically informed way of conceptualizing the problem at hand, an anticipated misunderstanding. I call Samantha's anticipation of the need to prepare, organize, and present information in the form of locutionary acts that help her achieve her intended illocutionary force with focus on a desired perlocutionary effect working *like* a linguist, as I will now explore.

The components that Austin uses to describe how meaning gets made in interaction provide a way in to consider how Samantha is doing things with language, aka working *like* a linguist.

Speech Act Theory:

- what is said (the form of the utterance or the locutionary act),

- the intended effect of this by the speaker (illocutionary force), and

- the observable effect on the listener (perlocutionary effect).

Samantha can foresee that no one is going to know what to do with the locutionary act, "I am a linguist," which will render her unable to have the desired impact on those assembled—the perlocutionary effect—of deciding to hire her. That is, using Austin's framework, illocutionary force (her intention) is to help attendees of Forward Fest recognize her value. Thus, to achieve the perlocutionary effect of a client deciding to hire her, she is designing additional locutionary acts (descriptions of examples of her work) to have at the ready.

After all, "I'm launching my business" is like the classic example "It's cold in here" of conventionalized indirectness. Samantha is not going to say, "Hire me!" just as we know that if someone says "Is it cold in here?" it may well mean "Turn up the heat" or "Shut that window," or "Go get me a sweater!" Thus, Samantha has set about doing all of the things that she possibly can—including having already launched the business before she says, "I'm launching the business"—to create the felicity conditions that will support the locutionary act "I'm launching my business" to have the desired perlocutionary effect.

In the next example, Samantha gives the details of an example project where she conducted linguistic register analysis for a client in the health and wellness space (Figure 1.1).

This is another way she does what she describes in Example 3, giving potential clients "a box for linguists."

Now, Samantha went on to do what she intended to do—she launched her business—but before I conclude this telling of her story, I want to address something that I often hear when I workshop these data.

In Example 3, her ambivalence is palpable in the discursive construction of ownership of the decision to launch.

Example 3 "Maybe I am ready for that!"

46.		and I hadn't even considered that idea like I didn't think I was ready for that.
47.		um but
48.	Anna Marie:	yep <nodding>
49.	Samantha:	but but when she told me,

50.		that I could do it and should do it, it made me think "wow, maybe I am ready for that!"
51.		and then I thought: "well, it's still like three months away" at that point like "maybe I can get ready for that"
52.		you know,
53.	Anna Marie:	smart.
54.	Samantha:	so like that's like my official launch event.

 Samantha Beaver, MA • 1st
Language Expert | Data Analyst | Corporate Trainer
1yr • 🌐

Tegan Peterson, owner of **Urban Rituals Spa LLC** (https://lnkd.in/dagVETV), centers her life and work-practice around physical and mental WELLNESS. But marketing and promoting wellness is a complicated linguistic task. Tegan, along with Memra Language Services, is using Linguistic Register Analysis to make sure that all of her linguistic choices will attract the right clients and communicate her central message. What message are YOU trying to communicate?

○ 4 • 1 Comment

👍 Like   💬 Comment   ↷ Share

FIGURE 1.1 *Samantha Beaver LinkedIn post—client work*

Her hedging displays the very real and very appropriate fear and uncertainty that accompany taking such a huge and important risk. But it is also relevant to know that one of Samantha's research interests—and one of the things Memra Language Services specializes in—is gendered talk at work. Her admission that she hadn't even considered the idea (line 46), her acknowledgment that it was the advice and encouragement of this mentor that made her think she was ready, and her use of "maybe," and the fact that she has to talk herself into it, comprise a collection of features that can get heard as non-agentive. In a business world that is shaped by expectations of self-presentation that get read as "confident," these ways of talking can get heard as ineffectual.

When in fact they are exactly the opposite. She did the thing. She launched the business.

I would argue that uncertainty and doubt are absolutely appropriate because they are reflective of reality. Certainty in career is impossible.

Certainty is a narrative by-product of narrating the past, and when stories about work get shared, they tend to be from people after they have already figured things out. This is another reason I think it crucial to hear stories from people in the midst of career transition.

People in the midst of career transition may not be inclined to share and don't tend to be invited to share their story in the midst of its unfolding. When I ask people in this state, they often say "no," seemingly fearing that it would be a bad thing to share their disorientation and confusion. But I suggest that as a field, we suffer from not hearing these stories, because their erasure has resulted in an internalization of the mistaken notion that everyone else has this career thing all sorted out (from the stories we hear, it seems like our uncertainty is abnormal!).

The reader may already be noticing that I have made the decision to oversample stories from women in this book. As a woman, I chose to do this as a corrective to the pattern of women's voices not being heard in various professional settings. This also includes ways of talking that get read as "feminine" and get misheard and misinterpreted, as we have just discussed.

In the process of creating the next story, Anne invited me to continue reckoning with my intentions to recognize another erasure. I saw that I could do more work to center the perspectives of other groups—particularly scholars of color—whose voices and experiences get actively silenced in broader society, and unfortunately also within the field of linguistics.

Anne Charity Hudley

Increasing Diversity in the Linguistic Sciences

Anne Charity Hudley is a professor of education at Stanford University and the Principal Investigator on a grant from the National Science Foundation (NSF) focused on Increasing Diversity in the Linguistic Sciences through Research on Language and Social Mobility.

When I last saw her in person, in January 2020 in New Orleans, LA—the same city where she had conducted her dissertation research—Anne was inviting our field into a conversation about race, racism, and racial justice as part of her invited plenary at the Linguistic Society of America (LSA) annual meeting. In collaboration with the LSA and along with co-authors Christine Mallinson, Mary Bucholtz, Nelson Flores, Nicole Holliday, Elaine Chun, and Arthur Spears, Anne had been recently developing a statement on race with the LSA. During her plenary, she invited feedback from the assembly to inform the article which subsequently appeared in *Language,* our field's flagship journal.

In telling her story here, I'll begin with these two pieces—the statement on race and the subsequent *Language* article—which argue for the need for an interdisciplinarily informed theoretical engagement with race and racism. I'll then situate these within the broader context of Anne's decades of work centering African-American language, reviewing the ways she has explored variation and change in this variety in order to advance access, equity, and inclusion in classrooms, institutions, and in society. I'll conclude with a glimpse at the social media advocacy she has been engaged in most recently, ending with a call to action she issued as part of a Facebook Live on Juneteenth: June 19, 2020.

In the statement on race, Anne and her co-authors invite the field into a reckoning with race and racism by noting how our sister fields (sociology, anthropology, and psychology) acknowledge that prejudice, discrimination, and racism remain profound social problems and that whether acknowledged or not, race is central to every aspect of academic knowledge production. As they argue, all research proceeds from a point of view, regardless of whether that is acknowledged, examined, denied, or suppressed. The authors point specifically to our failure as a discipline to engage with critical race theory, and the need for interrogating our methods and models for their racial inclusivity, seeking social and quantitative examinations of race that aim for social justice: "We should work towards models that more explicitly aim to empower (not just describe and value) voices" (Charity Hudley, Mallinson, et al., 2019: 4).

In the published response they go on to argue that "the lack of comprehensive and up-to-date theoretical, analytical, and political understandings of race within linguistics not only weakens research by erasing, marginalizing, and misrepresenting racially minoritized groups, but it also diminishes the impact of the entire field by devaluing and excluding the intellectual contributions of researchers of color" (Charity Hudley, Mallinson, et al., 2020: 1). They also point to institutional structures like "alienating undergraduate and graduate curricula; narrow definitions of excellence in admissions, hiring, and promotion decisions; and the constant policing both of what counts as linguistics and what counts as research" as factors that contribute to alienation and point to the need for substantial reparative and restorative work both within our field and among potential collaborators. For context, they point to the continued devaluing of language-related scholarship produced by such fields as communication, English, education, and applied linguistics (24), and the "simple but powerful acts" that linguists can do such as citing scholars of color in articles and research presentations, assigning their work in class, and including images and life histories; acknowledging and addressing rather than denying our discipline's role in the reproduction of racism. They call for engaging in anti-racist and inclusion-focused education in ways that promote equity in theory, practice, and teaching (25–6).

As part of her plenary at the LSA in January 2020, Anne described a promising recent project focused on fostering diversity in the linguistic sciences involving undergraduates from Historically Black Colleges and Universities (HBCUs) and other Minority-Serving Institutions

(MSIs), which do not offer linguistics as a major. She created a summer program where students learn about linguistics while learning about their own linguistic histories through guided research exploring the linguistic choices that underrepresented minority students make as they navigate higher education. Specifically, she explores the stances and orientations that speakers take up to African-American and Standard Englishes as part of their development as students. This much-needed rich insight into this variation, variability, and change provides understanding about the language and culture of African-American college students, which has direct implications for teaching and mentoring, benefitting not only colleges and universities, but also broader society. Her work contributes to the understanding of the role of language in social mobility, but also stands to increase diversity in the linguistic sciences.

In reflecting on an undergraduate research program that she directed at the College of William & Mary called WMSURE—the William & Mary Scholars Undergraduate Research Experience—Anne shares that although for a long time she had thought about the work of directing this program as separate from her identity as a linguist,

> I then realized that developing and directing the WMSURE was central to everything I do as a linguist as it was a direct way to contribute to inclusiveness in linguistics both by preparing individual students for graduate school and by creating a model of practice for linguistics faculty who teach undergraduates.

She invites faculty to think about how they might structure and include similar programming in order to advance inclusive excellence, locating undergraduate research as equity and inclusion work that academics can bring to their "own backyards."

By inviting her academic faculty colleagues—in their respective institutions—to analyze some of the ways that they might do better in engaging and supporting undergrads as part of bringing down some of the barriers to involvement which have existed in our field, I see Anne working *like* a linguist.

Consider this call in the journal *English Linguistics* to the linguistic disciplinary community to think about the broader scholarly and academic communities that we comprise:

I want to encourage the current, and next, generation of linguists to think about the comprehensive support of underrepresented undergraduate students as a main focus of the social justice mission of linguistics. We have had several generations of linguists who have shed light on the linguistic and social conditions of those who are marginalized in societies. Our response to that groundbreaking work is that we must now articulate a way for individuals from such backgrounds to enter our universities and succeed in linguistics. Otherwise, the hypocrisy in our work will ring apparent and our intellectual contributions will be markedly incomplete. Only through the concerted efforts of both individuals and groups of linguists, including departments, programs, and our professional organizations, including the LSA, will the diversity that is reflected in the languages that linguists study also be reflected in the students, faulty, and other researchers who study them. (211)

To support and structure this work, her future NSF funding will serve to bring university administrators into the conversation. Anne has also built a strong foundation designed to ensure lasting long-term impact by working extensively with K–12 educators in public and independent schools throughout the country.

I'll end this telling of Anne's story with a look at her social media advocacy where she shares ideas, encouragement, and resources to encourage speaking up for racial justice. As part of a Facebook Live broadcast during the summer of 2020, she gives a multilevel model for action, which considers the institutional level (How do our institutions support inclusion?), the social and family level (with resources like the Speak Up campaign of the Southern Poverty Law Center), the neighborhood and physical community level (asking 'Is my neighborhood a place where Black folks want to be? And if not, what can we do about that?'), and finally, the social media level. As she says:

Let's do this together
This is about collective bravery
Don't make it up as you go along
Read what people are recommending

To conclude here, I thought I would share how she closed out a call about standing up and speaking out:

> We got this!
> People are listening, people are watching,
> From politicians, to corporations, to educators,
> Put these action plans in place
> Get people in these conversations
> Think about what they want to do in a timely manner
> Pick something small if that's where you are
> Learn a little bit, ask a question
> Push further
> Ask bigger questions
> Demand change if you're in that place
> And please by any means speak out if you are in the position to do so
> We need your voices
> We need your signs
> We need that now to keep going!

A Story from Me: Thanking John Rickford

In her plenary, Anne shared that one of the research participants from her project with HSBCUs said to her, "Imagine if more of us knew!" (meaning, what a difference it could make if more speakers of African-American English were exposed to linguistic study of their language earlier in their studies), which sparked a memory for me about two of the students from an Introduction to Linguistics class I taught at Howard University in 2006. These students put together an event called "Got English?" for their English Language and Literature international honor society.

They pulled together students from all over the country and from different regions of the globe to celebrate English in its inherent variability. I remember laughing when they told me the event would start at 7:24 pm—but then learned this was a playful way to acknowledge their history as an association, Sigma Tau Delta, which was founded in 1924.

As I recall, it was the "five present tenses" quotation from Nobel Prize-winning author Toni Morrison that John and Russell Rickford use to begin their beautiful book *Spoken Soul* that had sparked Monica and Angela's interest in organizing this event in the first place:

> It's terrible to think that a child with five different present tenses comes to school to be faced with books that are less than his own language. And then to be told things about this language, which is him, that are sometimes permanently damaging. He may never know the etymology of Africanisms in his language, not even that "hip" is a real world or that "the dozens" meant something. This is a really cruel fall-out of racism. I know the standard English. I want to use it to help restore the other language, the lingua franca.

Monica and Angela taught their fellow students some of the things that they had been learning about syntax and morphology and sematic shift in their linguistics class, using as an example a recent discussion about the many meanings and purposes of the term "jont" in the African-American English spoken in Washington, DC.

In those early years when I was first teaching, *Spoken Soul* was one of my very favorite ways to invite curiosity about syntax. I'd love that spark of curiosity that I would see: "What do you mean five present tenses?" This book is a beautiful celebration of language and culture, and it is one of the best expressions of joy in art with language; I return to it—and recommend it—often.

Anne's story sparked this memory, which prompted me to send a gracious note to John Rickford and Russel Rickford (Figures 1.2 and 1.3) for their wonderful book. Our email exchange in turn prompted a discussion about a remarkable event kicking off just this week at the time of writing: the Linguistics Career Launch, organized by the convenors of a Special Interest Group (SIG) at the Linguistics Society of America called Linguistics Beyond Academia (LBA).

Their unprecedented and amazing accomplishment—a month-long career education event for linguists—has been the result of mindset shifts happening for many years in our field including efforts that Professor (John) Rickford had taken to acknowledge and stay in touch with his graduates who work in contexts beyond the academic which he shared with me in the form of a spreadsheet back when I was

FIGURE 1.2 *John Rickford—co-author of* Spoken Soul

the convenor of the LBA SIG. His many years of work fostering and maintaining relationships of trust between potential employers and academic institutions in turn supported my work, as I in turn have been supporting the efforts of the organizers of this event, and I'm so glad that I was reminded to thank him for that work, and give him a sense for where some of his efforts have led many years down the road!

And this is how I want you to be listening to the stories in this book, reader. See what sparks for you. Does a story give you an idea or remind you of something? Where can that take you? And then what?

I'll close out this chapter with an activity to get you started.

I'll ask you to think about books, conversations, ideas, research, and people that have sparked your interests. And as we close out Anne's story, if her work has sparked a curiosity for you, and you want to learn more about her work, as she says, she has enough online to keep anyone "busy for years" up at https://annecharityhudley.com/. There are resources for doing your homework—your reading homework, your connecting homework, and your organization

FIGURE 1.3 *Russel Rickford—co-author of* Spoken Soul

homework (religious groups, alumni associations, reputable groups like the American Civil Liberties Union, Anti-Defamation League, National Association for the Advancement of Colored People, Showing Up for Racial Justice, etc.)

A Catalyst for You: Finding Your Sparks

For many linguists, there was a moment where/when you realized that linguistics was the thing for you. If you have a moment like that, it's one of your sparks. For this activity, I'd like you to make some time to identify a few such moments, maybe three to five (enough so that you can start to see emerging patterns).

Make some time and space to get creative!

As you will see in my example below, I got out the colored pencils and some paper. My "Oh, it's linguistics!" moment is a visual memory, so you can see that I drew a little image of that in the top circle. Funnily enough, this memory was also a time when I took out the colored pencils, which may be why it sticks with me!

It was the final for my first linguistics class, and I had decided that the different colors would help me see (learn, remember) how Syntax, Semantics, Phonology, Morphology, and Pragmatics, etc. all interpolated. How these systems were embedded. I was taking this class as part of a year abroad at the Universidad de Costa Rica and at this point in the semester, my Spanish had seen a vast improvement over the course of several months. There was something about this muliticolored notecard that made me suddenly recognize how my own process of acquisition had unfolded in stages. That my ability to recognize these was supported by the labels linguistics was giving me to be able to describe them. I had realized that it had been continually happening that I would suddenly notice a mistake that I knew I had been making for months, but that I just hadn't been able to see until I got to some next level. My linguistics class had handed me a systems schematic for why this was happening—about how my brain worked—which I found to be simply intoxicating!

In the image below, you'll see that I started with that image and then chased ideas out and into a "big bang": people and opportunities which led me to be there in Costa Rica in the first place to even be able to make that notecard, and also what happened as a result (people and opportunities that took me to, which led to further ideas and decisions) (Figure 1.4).

Another bright star that guided me was Professor Deborah Schiffrin, who I was lucky enough to have been able to work with as both student and colleague at Georgetown University. In fact, her work, *Discourse Markers*, was the thing that brought me to Georgetown in the first place. Her former classmate Greg Guy, with whom I was working at New York University, had told me to look at it as a resource for the research paper I was doing about the discourse marker "pura vida,"

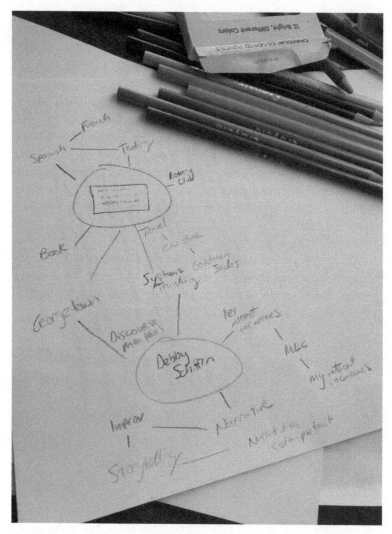

FIGURE 1.4 *Anna Marie Big Bang sketch (author's photograph)*

in Costa Rican Spanish. Because of this, I applied for and received a grant from the Tinker Foundation (whose mission is to promote the development of an equitable, sustainable, and productive society in Latin America) to return to Costa Rica to do some research while an MA student. And I have no doubt that having done an independent research project on that scale was a factor in the decision to accept me for a PhD.

I'm discovering/remembering these connections as I write about them—on the paper pictured in image in Figure 1.4, I had started to identify commonalities of narrative, storytelling, and Georgetown. Improv, which became the subject of my dissertation, was initially attractive to me as a creative and social outlet when I first moved to Washington, DC but ultimately drew me in and captured my imagination because it gave me a different kind of access to talking about the interpolated systems I was learning about in linguistics. This art form gave me access to the ways that other people's brains made connections, an interest in systems thinking, which continues to express itself.

What stories can you spark?

Save your notes, as we will be using the ideas that you generate throughout the book to chart a way forward for yourself. These sparks help you identify patterns to map out constellations and galaxies that will help you navigate your present and future career.

2

BRIGHTEN While You Work

The ten stories in this chapter feature ten linguistics students who took a professional development course with me in the Spring of 2011. Their engagement with the world of work illuminates some of the major sectors and ways in which linguists find application of our skills and training: Business, Research, Innovation, Government, Healthcare (Communication), Technology, Education, and the Nonprofit world. From their experience, I derived the acronym BRIGHTEN to capture and convey the breadth and range of professional possibilities for linguists. I also wanted to have a ready answer to the question, "What can linguists do?" that was not only explanatory, but deliberately positive. I sought to invoke a "growth," rather than a "fixed" mindset (Dweck, 2007) when it comes to work. "BRIGHTEN" also works well within the metaphorical domain of "stars" and continues the themes of energy and sparking that we have begun exploring in the first chapters.

Like stars, their stories illuminate. Top among the themes they reveal is change. Ten years after graduating with their MA degrees, they have gotten married, had children, moved, moved back, gone back for their PhDs and yes, they have changed jobs. Unlike their parents or grandparents, people currently beginning their careers are extremely unlikely to have the same job for thirty years. In fact, over the course of collecting these stories, many of them lost or changed their roles, and I heard from many of them that they fully expect to have many roles beyond their current one. The stamp of late-market capitalism is unmistakable in this picture of change, which might just as easily be called precarity as entrepreneurial. As a descriptive researcher, my aim here is not to endorse the state of hyper-capitalism (Gonick and Kasser, 2018) in which we currently find ourselves, but rather by documenting and describing these systems, to give those of us who must engage with them something of a better sense of our own agency, choice, and power.

The professional experiences of these linguists also illuminate some broad patterns about the world of work generally, including the interconnections across sectors, permeability and fluidity across some of the perceived barriers or central dualities—working "inside" and "outside" academia, working for yourself, and working for an employer, or indeed paid and unpaid labor (hopefully inviting a bit of reflection about what gets valued and remunerated in our society). Their stories also touch upon themes that tend to come up in career conversations among and about linguists, including working as part of a team of linguists and working as the only linguist at an organization, working as a nontechie in tech, and again, working *as* or working *like* a linguist. Only a couple of these professionals have the title "linguist"—and in some cases, it is the broader meaning of the term employed by the military—but every one of them works *like* a linguist. My argument is that their training as linguists shows up in how they work, and that this is valuable: to the linguist, to their employer, and to the world.

With each, I focus on an aspect of their work today that I view as being directly connected to their training, a task that I am aided in by virtue of having been a part of their education ten years ago. However, as I make these connections, I invite you, reader, to draw your own. Take from my vantage point the utility of perspective. The fact that I can see breadth of possibility is an invitation to do so yourself.

Finally, a quick note about process. I mentioned in Chapter 1 that the form and context of stories were interactionally emergent. In this chapter, I used the linguist's LinkedIn profile to craft the first draft of the story, and sent it along with an invitation to discuss further—not only to smooth out the exuberances and deficiencies inherent in storytelling, but also to get feedback on the connections I was drawing—the links that I saw. The meaning I derive from their experiences is undeniably my own, but I do very much want for it to also be recognizable to the person whose experience I am narrating.

They might not have drawn the link in the way that I did, but once I had drawn it, I hoped that it resonated. As it happened, my timing coincided with shelter-in-place orders around the Covid-19 pandemic of 2020, making it in some ways slightly easier to get in touch with everyone, and in so doing practice what I preach about staying in contact with the members of your professional networks.

So, now to BRIGHTEN and how it helps to illuminate work.

It is convenient that the acronym starts with business, because of these ten linguists, many of them currently work or have worked in what might be called the "business sector," including such marquee organizations as Johnson and Johnson, Nike, Comcast, and Google. At the same time, the multitude of "ways in" that they found, and the observable variety among the things that they actually do as part of their work in this sector—not to mention the similarity to work done in other sectors—belie the enormity and diversity of business, and thus really begin the conversation exactly where we would want it to: by revealing ambiguity and complexity.

B of BRIGHTEN: Business

I'll start with Carolyn. Having just mentioned that employees nowadays are unlikely to be at one organization for the entirety of their professional lives, Carolyn's experience gives us a bit of texture to this observation. She—unlike most of her classmates—was in fact at the same organization for much of this decade we are chronicling— for seven years. However, as we'll see, she spent this time actively seeking opportunities to grow and develop, to pursue opportunities to learn and have new experiences, and she did not stay at the organization once she realized that she wanted something different.

Although her career path moves in and out of many of our pieces of the BRIGHTEN acronym, Carolyn's work can be described as being squarely within Business because of the clients that she works with (global financial institutions, pharmaceutical brands, and the technology and entertainment sectors) as well as the explicit nature of her work being that of growing the business (for her own organization or for clients). However, the specific way that she grows business—makes money—is by designing and marketing methods and products featuring linguistic analysis. As she says, "linguistics is often shiny and new for people."

Along with another classmate Kathryn—whose work we will hear more about in the R for Research and the H for Healthcare Communication sections of the acronym—Carolyn began her professional life working as an analyst of Linguistic Insights for a research agency in the healthcare communications space called Verilogue. After spending two years as an analyst, she got promoted to senior analyst, and then was entrusted with management responsibilities. One thing to note here is that although her title was "manager" she was not managing people, which may be important for readers to know—contrary to popular understanding, you don't have to manage people to be successful and "rise in the ranks" in a business setting.

Eventually, when an opportunity presented to go do business development (or as she puts it, "sell the secret sauce") for the Paris office, Carolyn leapt at the chance to have an opportunity to live and work abroad. As a "Global Business Development Representative" (in this context, "development" means sales) Carolyn was responsible for pitching language and language analysis, which—since many people aren't really thinking about language in the ways that we do as linguists—was exciting and fresh to many potential clients.

Ultimately, however, she realized that sales was not for her ("bring me in once you have the meeting" is how she put it) and she decided to come back to be closer to home and closer to her research interests, so she returned to be the Associate Director of the Linguistic Insights team, leading the development of a new research methodology, cognitive interviewing, among other initiatives. Three years later, she became the Director of Linguistics and Innovation, and at the time of writing has recently left the organization to pursue voice research for Comcast, touching the R for Research and T for Technology parts of our acronym.

Carolyn wanted readers to know that this last transition took nearly a year of self-reflection. She had been feeling burned out and stagnant in her job, and although she needed to continue working full-time, she wanted to give herself the time and space to explore the best next move. She made as much mental space as she could to be productively disoriented—harkening back to the theme we explored in Chapter 1 (and as we will revisit in Chapter 4)—and I appreciate her reminder that there are lots of forms that "productive disorientation" can take. In his excellent book, *The Originals*, Adam Grant reminds us that the myth of the big dramatic quit and leap into the great unknown is precisely that: a myth. Most of us—not even the entrepreneurs who are supposed to be fearless—can really afford to take on that much risk. Career change is an incremental and iterative, often gradual process.

To sum up, although Carolyn was originally hired specifically for her linguistic analytic toolkit (she has after all worked in two among the few sectors that recruit linguists explicitly—healthcare communications research and voice-user interface—sectors whose job ads often directly ask for training in syntax, semantics, phonology, morphology, etc.), she has thrived in her professional roles by being a good partner (and thus ensuring/inviting repeat business), and by understanding the market so as to be able to identify where the opportunities are. In early roles, this involved marketing—speaking to the user base in a way that resonated. Now, it involves touching all aspects of the "customer journey."

Having been the person who taught her ethnography of communication, I can draw a direct line from the observation and professional listening that she did as part of her final project in that class (observing how language functions in the socialization which takes place over the course of an executive MA degree in Business), to her work now observing how language functions at each point in the customer journey: from the words and phrases that entice new customers, to the ways of communicating that best get them set up to use their products or services, to the linguistic elements of troubleshooting, to "delighting them" as users of a product.

Corporate Social Responsibility

Renee's path within the B for Business sector is somewhat unique, for one thing because she is an athlete, which was how she landed her first internship at Nike. As an organization, Nike prefers to hire folks highly familiar with qualities of teamwork and collaboration that involvement with sports cultivates. When Nike offered her the opportunity to design an internship tailored to her interests, Renee carved out a project for herself on the communications team as the Global Brand Communications Intern, doing things like collecting ethnographic data for organizational communications analysis, and conducting qualitative media analysis on communications campaigns to offer "next step" insights and solutions. From this beginning, Renee found her way into working with Johnson and Johnson on Corporate Social Responsibility (CSR) initiatives, which included research into birth asphyxia, soil transmitted helminths, and the frontline healthcare worker movement.

She notes an increase in focus on metrics and evaluation to measure impact within CSR, and observes that her training as a linguist to be flexible and adaptable with methodology has been invaluable. I have heard from many linguists that one of our superpowers is that of selecting and adapting tool to task. In Renee's case, her ability to adopt both traditional and nontraditional methodologies to evaluate effectiveness of programs, grants, and partnerships has yielded rich insight and been valuable to her employers, clients, partners, and other stakeholders.

For example, when she came back to the MLC program a few years after she graduated to talk to current students, Renee talked about a current global health initiative for which her responsibilities included "partner relationship management" (being in regular communication both internally and external to the organization), which occasioned the following observation:

> Although I may not necessarily be capitalizing on my background in Linguistics in all day-to-day job tasks (i.e., transcription, discourse analysis, semiotic analysis) I operate daily within the mindset of a linguist. With a heightened awareness of how language and communication operate within particular communities of practice, I am able to quickly adapt to various workplaces and work styles. I also draw on my education in language and communication to explain and dissect miscommunications or mis-aligned expectations within the workplace and come up with solutions. Being a linguist with a background in language and communication helps me to understand why an organization operates the way it does, and how to best contribute to the shared mission.

Over the years, Renee has maintained her focus on athletics and is now a professional athlete for the USA Triathalon.

You Don't Have to Pick One!

As part of the Proseminar course, I asked students to "pick one" (one organization, one sector, one professional interest, etc.) so as to be able to focus their interests and move forward with the job search. I found that choosing one area to focus on was a useful way to engender momentum for many of my students, but Matt never could pick just one interest. He was interested in many things, including healthcare communications and advocacy. He had worked earlier in supporting people with autism. But he was also interested in forensic linguistics, linguistics and music, regional variation, and dialectology. The more he looked into something, the more it seemed to interest him, and I finally had to accept that he wouldn't "pick one," which turned out to be the perfect attribute for the direction his path ended up taking, that of proposal writer.

To be a proposal writer, you must be broadly interested in many sectors to be able to see the needs of the individual parties and be able to bridge those needs with the services offered by the organization offering to meet them. Writing proposals has enabled Matt to engage with clients from the government, technology, and nonprofit sectors, and even to bring the skills he has been cultivating in the business world—research and writing, content development— to be able to serve as volunteer for Respect/Ability—a public policy organization that enables him to do advocacy work for individuals with disabilities—work that he deeply values. In addition, Matt's work in proposal writing sometimes dovetails with his linguistic interests. His proposal background recently enabled him to (tangentially) revisit his passion for healthcare-related communication when he took a proposal writing position at MAXIMUS, an organization specializing in health and human services support, with particular focus on medicaid enrollment and marketing (including mitigating language barriers for residents in various states).

I believe it was from Professor Rob Podesva, my colleague at Georgetown, that I first heard that "linguistics is where top-down meets bottom-up," and I see that characteristic in Matt's emergent career path. The bottom-up piece of the equation is in the careful research and writing he must do to develop content for proposals. He must also be particularly good at framing the big picture—identifying the alignment between what an organization needs and what his client organization offers. If he can get the balance right, the person for whom he is writing the proposal gets the gig (or the funding, makes the sale). No matter what field, sector, or industry, proposals are an important way that work and goods get assigned: one organization needs something done, another offers to do it. Matt's role, right there in the middle is to identify the best way of clearly conveying "this is what this is all about"—in other words: framing.

R of BRIGHTEN: Research

Many of the ten linguists from the Proseminar do—or have done—research as part of their work, including all four of the stories I have shared thus far. And, one of the most interesting things about research is that when you start to talk about it in the work context, it brings you immediately back to business, because everything about the ways that research work gets done has everything to do with the organizational structure, sector, and relationship of the researcher/ research team to the institution.

Some organizations are entirely structured around conducing and communicating research: Knology in New York, for example, or Community Marketing Research and Insights, an organization that focuses solely on research and insights with the LGBTQ+ community. Holly found a career in research that has taken her through a variety of roles both in and outside the academy. And this ken for research was expressing itself even as an MA student; she sought out a role as a researcher for the Berkley Center for Religion, Peace, and World Affairs. In a program that did not require a research thesis, she was one of two (out of her cohort of ten) who decided to write one. Holly started her professional career after grad school at a research consultancy in the DC area called Fors Marsh, but then because her family moved to Colorado, she found work in the research department of a school district, where she worked to improve federally funded programs through qualitative research and using human-centered design to evaluate and improve program efficacy. For example, she created design-thinking workshops for Title I staff to use survey data to inform school-level changes for their family engagement initiatives.

Holly continues to be a researcher now as she has made the choice to go back for her PhD. She is in the Information Sciences Department at Indiana University, Bloomington—her tagline on LinkedIn reflects how her interests interrelate: "Sociolinguist & Information scientist investigating social interaction & technology." In her coursework as a Master's student, she consistently explored contexts of technology use and how they get used in the construction of identity (live action role playing games [LARPGs] and Twitter being just two examples). Now, as a PhD student, she seems to have reversed the polarity: and it is now about centering language in how technology gets used in oder to inform design; for example, how users change the way they use language when they adopt new technologies (e.g., a smart speaker like Alexa). Holly has always been very tenacious in finding the right fit for her. And whether she's bringing tech to linguistics or bringing linguistics to tech, her determination and conviction that a nuanced understanding of language and communication can enrich how we engage with technology will serve her—and serve the world—well.

I of BRIGHTEN: Innovation

Over the course of developing and using the BRIGHTEN acronym, the "I" has changed several times. Initially, I considered that it could stand for "Industry" because I heard this term bandied about by academics as a broad way of talking about work outside of academia. I wanted to complicate our use of this term (I perceive an embedding of the deictic center of the academy in this term, pointing to "industry" as "outside"). Because I adhere to a policy of "if you don't believe it, don't repeat it!" I decided that I did not want to further use of a referring term that I believe to be unhelpful.

So, to reflect the changing realities of work arrangements—and possibly because I was reading books like Daniel Pink's *Free Agent*

Nation and Pamela Slim's *Escape From Cubicle Nation*—I decided that the "I" could stand for "Independent." Later, I considered that it could talk about "internships," being that they are an important way that people gain experience in work and try out a possible interest. Ultimately, I decided to use "I" to bring "Innovation" into this conversation for its descriptive potential for capturing a quality of what linguists bring to (organizational) problem-solving.

Think about Charlotte Linde from Chapter 1: NASA reached out to her the first time because they recognized something innovative about her approach. Later, when she came back to NASA years later, she framed her expertise as belonging to the world of knowledge management. Because we interrogate assumptions—especially including truisms like "this is how we have always done this"—we linguists will always be innovative.

I think about Steven—from the group of ten in the Proseminar—who knew that he wanted to work in social change advocacy. He ended up landing an internship at the Center for American Progress, to whom he pitched an innovative analytical approach. As part of the Proseminar, students had to create a portfolio piece that showcased some aspect of their work. Steven fleshed out an analysis of the impact of pronoun use in fundraising appeals and other messaging, finding that use of "we" yielded more donor contributions. This got the organization intrigued, and once he was hired, he developed and gave trainings to his colleagues in the effective use and research of language in social media. This experience set him up for his next job as a digital strategist and linguistic analyst, and it also catalyzed a move into another sector, as we will hear about in the next section.

G of BRIGHTEN: Government

From the Center for American Progress, Steven moved to an organization called Well and Lighthouse LLC, a digital strategy firm that focuses on supporting political candidates, bringing narrative analytical techniques to bear on their campaigns. Political communications are but one of the many ways that linguists can and are engaging with the work of government.

I'll close this chapter with the story of how I came to work at the FrameWorks Institute, because of this cohort of students challenging me to do an ethnography of my own, but for now, I'll just mention that over the course of working with FrameWorks for many years I have had the opportunity to work with many government clients, and/or participate in work sponsored by government grants or public initiatives, including a recent project in adolescent substance use and abuse funded by SAMHSA—the Substance Abuse and Mental Health Services Administration. My role in that project was to support grantees—many of them housed in Departments of Health or Health and Human Services—to use the framing strategies developed by my colleagues on the research team at FrameWorks. In a work arrangement called "technical assistance"—a term used widely in the government sector to refer to consultation using specialized expertise—I build communications capacity in using storytelling for social change. For the SAMSHA project, I helped grantees use explanatory metaphors, storytelling structures, and other frame elements to communicate the need for and impact of substance use prevention work in ways that invoke collective social and civic responsibility.

Holly—who we met earlier—worked for a time in the public sector—as part of a Title I grant for a public school district, and earlier, with Fors Marsh, the research firm in Washington, DC, with many government clients (the Department of Veterans Affairs, Joint Advertising Marketing Research & Studies—the marketing branch of the military). In the environs of the District of Columbia, contracting with the government is quite common. Zara, for example, is a linguist whose research work supports a government client, and she has been working in this sector since she was a student. One of the many daily tasks she might perform in the course of her work is to assess thousands of media inputs in multiple languages, summarizing them for interpretation and use in policy decision-making. Zara often finds herself subtitling videos or translating texts to support the work of interpreting media streams—and nowadays, social media presence forms an important part of the analysis.

At her previous job at Georgetown University, Zara's research and writing responsibilities involved publishing or approving ten to forty analytical reports daily for use by the US intelligence, defense, homeland security, and public health communities. Later, she worked as principal editor for Magharebia, a website and news service for North Africa that used to be published in Arabic, English, and French by the United States African Command (AFRICOM), operated under General Dynamics Information Technology, a major government contractor. Magharebia was a public diplomacy effort designed for North African youth to provide an antiterrorist perspective to deter them from joining jihadist or other terrorist groups, an initiative of the Defense Department. Although cited as an example of best practices in this diplomacy sphere (Seib, 2010), the project lost its funding and so Zara moved over to an Intelligence Agency where she worked the overnight shift for almost two years. Her work there involved preparing briefings for a range of clients including federal agencies (among them the White House, the FBI, and the Department of Transportation) and companies in the energy and health sectors. Since 2016, she has been supporting just one federal agency as a contractor, and the workload is more like three to ten reports a week, done in close collaboration with teammates. This arrangement better suits her current work–life balance needs as a mom with young kids.

According to Zara, skills such as her "heightened awareness of linguistic, sociocultural and political factors worldwide" are particularly valued in this sector. Her lived experience as a first-generation immigrant gives her a depth of knowledge about cultural contexts and language variation among dialects of Arabic. Her aim is to identify drivers of change, and if we think about linguistics broadly as being the study of change, her courses in sociolinguistics, intercultural communication, the ethnography of communication, linguistics and education, and language teaching cultivated many analytical skills directly applicable to this work.

While there are none from this particular cohort who happen to hold public office, or work for a federal agency, a contemporary of theirs from a different MA program now works as an instructional designer and trainer at the US Senate. In addition to delivering senate-specific trainings in the District of Columbia and State offices, she also conducts needs assessments to determine what trainings are needed, as well as evaluations to explore their effectiveness. In Chapter 6, we will also hear from Andrea Drew about her career working for the Central Intelligence Agency (CIA).

H of BRIGHTEN: Healthcare Communication

The skills and training of linguistics are specifically sought by many organizations in the healthcare communications sector. Take, as an example, this description of essential duties from a recent job posting for a Linguistic Analyst at Verilogue:

- Analyze conversations between healthcare professionals and patients.

- Synthesize linguistic patterns into coherent and meaningful insights for client marketing research teams.

- Advocate research findings to internal and client audiences through written reports (PowerPoint) and in-person presentations.

Kathryn has worked for many organizations in the sector, and currently in the capacity of Research Director for InVibe Labs, she "helps healthcare organizations better understand their customers by capturing authentic stories and translating sound science into actionable insights." As Research Director, Kathryn spends significant time with clients and has found a variety of powerful ways to describe the linguistic "value-add." In other words, why they need linguists. She sometimes describes herself as "human-centered design specialist with a background in communication, ethnography and voice analysis." As she explains, training in linguistics enables us to "uncover in-depth insights and make meaningful recommendations for a variety of clients."

Kathryn interfaces with the tech sector a great deal as part of her work. Not only does she use analytical techniques to draw insights from big corpora and data sets, she also participates in tech conferences, and writes for industry publications including *PharmaVoice*. I found this piece that she shared in the November/December edition particularly interesting. Kathryn had been selected for a feature titled "Data Scientists: Tomorrow's Pharma Superhero?" in which she challenged the very premise of the question by re-centering social science. As she shared: "Long maligned with words like 'softer' or 'subjective' social science is quickly gaining traction as a critical element within pharma's ongoing research priorities." She goes on to argue: "We can, and should, work to make healthcare technology more humanizing for patients and clinicians alike by focusing ways to capture the stories that give meaning to our lives." In this piece, she was reflecting on EHRs—electronic health records—but the potential applications of this observation are myriad.

T of BRIGHTEN: Technology

So, now that we are into talking about technology, let's turn for a moment to the "Tech for Good" movement, which prioritizes human well-being in design, development, and growth. Rather than letting economic factors like labor reduction or cost savings through automation be the drivers for thinking and decision-making (or innovation for innovation's sake), what would it mean to ask questions about quality of life, such as "Is this technology designed to addict us and therefore degrade our quality of life?" As we linguists increasingly move into the sector, we need to bring our ways of thinking to challenge assumptions as we engage with and inform the work. Especially if we don't think of ourselves as particularly tech-savvy, we are well positioned to keep analytical distance and help the sector keep well-being top of mind, and focus on the potential for technology to empower communities and bring benefit.

I hear from many linguists who are interested in the tech sector, but worry that they are not "techie" enough. If this describes you, I'd love it if the one thing you take away from reading this book is this: as social scientists we are uniquely trained to be aware of the broader social contexts. The tech sector especially needs more of this awareness, even if it isn't what they are asking for in job ads. We can and must stay cognizant of the bigger problems to innovate potential solutions.

Elvira's first major job after grad school was Junior Linguist at Google. As she describes it, when she started the MA program in Linguistics, she thought she wanted to focus on Cross-Cultural Communication facilitation, but was open to exploring other areas of linguistic application. She applied for every job that seemed to fit her skill set and ended up in the tech field, using her language skills in Russian as a data analyst. Because it was a former classmate who recommended her, she says that she sometimes feels as though her break into the tech world was by chance, but her story also demonstrates more than a small degree of tenacity. She came into the work as a contractor with the staffing and recruiting firm Adecco, through which many of the folks who contract at Google are sourced. This reflects a bigger reality of hiring done by many firms in the technology sector and means that Elvira worked without guaranteed employment, health insurance, or regular employee status within the organization, in the hope of gaining experience that would be attractive to an employer willing to offer full employment and benefits down the road.

While in her case, it worked out exactly the way she hoped it would, the systemic implications of this hiring trend are far-reaching and merit further reflection, discussion, and call for significant structural change. While beyond the scope of this discussion, and not in the hands of any one jobseeker, capitalism shapes processes that we can't avoid in the modern workforce (even for those working within the nonprofit or academic sectors—all systems operate within these operant social structures), so we should not take them for granted nor think of ourselves as immune. Nor are we powerless.

For me, it's always yes—and! Yes, most of us need to have work to survive AND our economic and labor systems and policies are designed by people. We all get to decide how we are going to participate in their redesign to make them work better for everyone.

For many people looking to "get their foot in the door," contracting can be a great way to get some experience. The experience is presented to employees as an opportunity to be entrepreneurial, but the arrangement largely benefits the employer. The precarity is borne by the employee, and I know more than one person who bore the expenses of moving for a job, only to be let go a few months later, before being able to earn back the expenses incurred. In my own professional path, I have been a contingent employee many times. My very first professional role in fact was as a temp in the financial sector. During the transition between my MA and deciding whether to apply for a PhD I worked again as a temp for about nine months, and then I worked as an adjunct instructor while I was getting the PhD and have adjuncted many times since.

Yes, there are benefits to employees, as was the case for Elvira—the experience gave her an opportunity to try on a new role in a new sector and begin to understand what she, as a linguist, could contribute, without having to make a huge upfront commitment. The arrangement also afforded her some flexibility when she wanted to take time to have a family. In my case, it has enabled me to plug into work in a new city before I had many professional connections on more than one occasion—and I deeply value the experience that I gained and the relationships I made. But at the same time, there was a way in which I internalized that feeling of precarity, not knowing how long I would have the position, not having access to the resources of regular employees, worrying about the cost of covering things like health insurance, especially during US political administrations when leaders publicly stated their intention to get rid of any social supports like access to healthcare. These factors made me anxious, which affected my ability to do my work—which compels me to mention it here. Engaging with the world of work means that we have an opportunity to reflect on what is important to us, and to bring an awareness of our own value, worth, and ability as we look for opportunities to either reify and reproduce systems or change them to meet the needs of the humans they are designed for.

To close out Elvira's story, what mattered most to her was work–life balance, and she was able to leverage her Google experience into an arrangement with a technology company called HERE Technology who specialize in geospatial mapping data. Elvira does annotation work for them that involves language skills (Russian language), and she's hoping to get back into the AI field and do linguistic data analysis work someday. For the time being, it's important for her to be able to work remotely and have a flexible schedule so that she can dedicate time to her children.

Let me just conclude this section on technology by saying that my time living in the environs of Silicon Valley has taught me that there seem to be abundant opportunities for linguists who want to get into AI work, and we will in fact hear a few stories in the chapters that follow from linguists who have done so. Everything that I have learned about the sector leaves me convinced that the most powerful thing that linguists bring to tech is our ability to see contexts and systems and make connections that help to challenge the status quo. The sector needs more people who see beneath assumptions, and who ask "why." I see many opportunities for Elvira to pursue her original interest in cross-cultural communication facilitation as the organizational culture—including diversity, equity, and inclusion—challenges facing the tech sector seem to be pernicious, tenacious, persistent, and unfortunately quite widespread.

E of BRIGHTEN: Education

As was the case with the discussion about "Research," so too for "Education" many linguists—particularly those who have a background in teaching—find a range of professional expression for teaching skills in curriculum design, facilitation, and training. What I like about Elizabeth's story is that it touches on many different combinations and applications of linguistics and education, and her experience and interests model various ways in which these two fields can be combined.

When I caught up with Elizabeth, she was working as adjunct faculty teaching English as a Second Language (ESL), English, English Composition, and Linguistics at Porterville College in Porterville, California. She had also recently started a new volunteer position as Bakersfield's Municipal Liaison for Nanowrimo (National Novel Writing Month), and was doing research into possibilities for working in educational technology (Ed Tech).

And I don't mean to be too "meta," but it was very easy to see connections back to her training because in her case, she was having her Porterville College students do one of the very same activities we did in the Proseminar: bringing discourse analysis to the task of identifying and analyzing keywords to create tailored resumes and cover letters. As we had done, she asked her students to feed the text of a particular job announcement into a word cloud generator and then consider how to represent key concepts in the design of their resume and cover letter materials in response. Words that appear with great frequency in a job ad ought to appear frequently in a cover letter as well, but there are structural considerations: what must come first?

When she and I touched base six months later, the Fall semester was just beginning, and she was thinking about how she might sneak in some more concepts from linguistics that would help her freshmen learn English Composition. One of my mentors, Deborah Schiffrin (who we heard about earlier in the book), used to like to say that people were either "lumpers" or "splitters"—that is, they tend to be looking for ways to combine ideas or ways to organize them by their differences. At this point in the telling of her tale, I think it is safe to say that Elizabeth is a lumper!

And that quality stands to take her places—for example, for her next pivot into Ed Tech, she's focusing particularly on organizations that express a value for the classroom experience that she brings as well as the work that she did at the Center for Applied Linguistics (CAL) developing curriculum and resources, evaluating assessment standards, and conducting teacher training. Organizations that seem to value these skills include ABC Mouse, The Art of Problem Solving, IXL Learning, and No Red Ink.

As she was reflecting on our current reality—in which all of her teaching is being done online—she sees direct parallels to the work she did in assessment, where she had to think a lot about clear communication with students in an asynchronous environment. Presupposition, for example, is a useful tool for thinking about how shared knowledge shapes how we talk to our students, assign work, give feedback. As in just about any context, meta-talk is very useful.

N of BRIGHTEN: Nonprofit

I featured Hollis's first five years on the job closely in *Bringing Linguistics to Work*, chronicling the close and trusting working relationship that she had cultivated with her manager. I was impressed with how collaboratively they navigated her professional development in choosing opportunities for her within Reading Partners, the literacy nonprofit where she landed after graduate school. Hollis came to the organization with a background in philanthropy, specifically fundraising and grant writing or "development" as they call it in the nonprofit sector, and when she eventually left Reading Partners, it was this deep background in development that helped her land a gig at a dream organization, National Public Radio (NPR). When we left off with her story in *Bringing Linguistics to Work*, Hollis had started a job with the Catalogue for Philanthropy that afforded her a bit more flexibility and work–life balance as she started a family. She has since moved with her family to Colorado, where the whole family is enjoying more work–life balance and more time with family, community, and nature.

Many factors can pull our focus to the structural conditions of our work, and in Hollis's case, that pull had been particularly strong and unusually focused. Her father is a career counselor, which has perhaps spurred a lifetime of career introspection, but I continue to marvel at how thoughtfully she uses both positive and negative experiences to consistently and regularly reflect and continue to move toward the things about which she is curious. She recently pursued her longstanding interest in teaching to undergo accreditation in the Montessori tradition. Ultimately, this ended up not being the right fit for her, but she knows that she fully immersed herself, so she never has to wonder "what if?" She has found the perfect fit for her in the remote work that she does as a contract writer for the George Kaiser Family Foundation and as a Director at Thread Strategies, where she draws on her research training to support small- to mid-sized nonprofits in assessing their current fundraising strengths and weaknesses. She draws on myriad linguistic frameworks including audience design, framing, and semantics to help partners "develop the strategies and tactical plans needed to raise more and more loyal dollars to support their missions."

We'll move now to a story from me, occasioned by these ten linguists in fact, and we'll also use some of the themes emerging from their work journeys including curiosity and agency to shape the activity that will close the chapter—that of job crafting.

A Story from Me: "Why Don't You Do an Ethnography?"

This group stands out in my memory because of the breadth and width of the interests they explored as part of the course, and also because they challenged me to put my money where why mouth is by doing my own ethnography. When I explained the assignment—that each student would choose an organization of interest—I explained that we would all benefit from everyone being as wide-reaching and far-ranging in their curiosity, because the more each student was able to find, the more knowledge we would all gain in turn. I encouraged them to do as much participant observation as possible—getting "inside the doors" of the organization if possible, for an informational interview or an event (whether virtual or in person). And when they put the challenge to me, I accepted and got to work seeking opportunities to engage with the FrameWorks Institute, an organization that I had been curious about for years.

The first connection that I found was a book reading at Politics and Prose bookstore of one of FrameWorks' employees, Michael Erard. His book *Babel No More* (featuring research and stories about hyperpolyglots—people who speak more than eleven languages) had just come out. Normally, I would have felt shy to go up and strike up a conversation with an author after the event, but because I knew that I had to share something in class, I challenged myself, and of course that one conversation led to many more, and he had ideas for me of other people to reach out to and other questions to ask. The more I learned about their work as an applied social science research firm, the more I was intrigued, and ultimately, all of this activity ended up culminating in my being at the right place and time when they needed to fill a position on the learning team (a new unit that had just been created). My obvious interest in their work and the fact that I knew a few folks who worked there by that point showed that I was very interested, and knowing what I knew about their work made me better prepared for the job interview as well.

So I can speak from experience when I say that this approach pays off! Having experienced how self-reflection and building community creates opportunities, I can recommend it wholeheartedly. And not just when job-seeking, this is something that professionals should be doing throughout their careers—because you never know what opportunity you might spark.

A Catalyst for You: Job Crafting

You always have choices as you navigate career.

If you currently have a job, you can always invest in continuing to develop it, looking for ways to bring it more into alignment with your current abilities, needs, and expectations, before you start the process of looking for a new one. Amy Wrzesniewski's body of research explores how "job crafting" can be a powerful tool for reenergizing and reimagining your work life, "redefining your job to incorporate your motives, strengths, and passions." As she and her collaborators explain, "The exercise prompts you to visualize the job, map its elements, and reorganize them to better suit you" (Wrzesniewski, Berg, et al., 2010).

Look closely at your tasks, the nature or extent of your interactions with other people, and think about how you might want to change part or whole—and this can happen in stages: maybe starting with reframing just for yourself, and then eventually with your colleagues, and finally in conversation with your manager. If you're self-employed, convene a group of other self-employed folks to hold you accountable for the changes that you want to make.

Job crafting may be a particularly important exercise for linguists on the job because often—especially when we work with managers who are not linguists—there could be more of a linguistic lens that we would want to bring to our work. Once you have been on the job a while and have built some trust and respect with your colleagues and team, there may well be room to push for adding something like:

- a research project or a writing component—maybe you see a newsletter as a chance to reconnect with the recent literature on your unique interests and perspective,

- some new technology that you want to learn that would expand your research capabilities, and/or

- maybe you want to get a linguistics student as an intern, or do more mentoring.

Over the years, I have asked for all of these, and they helped me bring more linguistics into the work that I do.

Ideally, you are working with a supervisor who will allow you to scale back on other aspects of the job—those which are less suited to your strengths—as you add others which are, but job crafting is a process, the course of which does not always run smooth. There may be an initial period in which you have more on your plate, until a way can be found to help you have less, but usually, adding in things that make you happier is worth the (hopefully temporary) discomfort.

And when and if it isn't, or if you find that you unfortunately have an employer who isn't interested in helping you grow in your work, well, then maybe it is time to think about what you want to try next!!

The best place to start may very well not be job advertisements. Both of the books that are in highest recommendation rotation in my catalogue these days, *Designing Your Life* and *What Color is Your Parachute?*, recommend that you instead begin by thinking about what the ideal job might be for you. Craft an ideal position for yourself and bring it to people who might want to hire you to do it. Both books are full of stories of people who have done just that, and who report great job satisfaction afterward because the job is a better fit from the outset, which only stands to reason.

3

HOW Linguists BRIGHTEN

In *Bringing Linguistics to Work*, the book I self-published in 2017, I shared a handful of stories about linguists at work. But now, thinking with the BRIGHTEN acronym, and the breadth and range of work contexts therein comprised—Business, Research, Innovation, Government, Healthcare Communication, Technology, Education, and Nonprofit—I realize that I somewhat oversampled Education in that book. True, the exploration did comprise many worlds of work: There was Holly Richardson, who undertook intensive career exploration upon completing her MA degree by identifying the range of local nonprofit organizations that supported the work of literacy acquisition. For Marc Okrand, it was discovering that managing in the context of his job in the Federal Government felt very much like teaching. For Caroline Latterman, the consulting that she did in Business contexts felt like teaching and was an expression of her commitment to raising awareness of language variation and connecting it to social justice by making visible the ways in which social meaning is constructed and construed through language. Finally, Aviad Eilam's breadth of experience as a language teacher led him to instructional design and curriculum development for an online learning platform. Later, his background in linguistics was recognized as an asset by Berlitz—a well-known language education company—that was willing to give him the chance to apply his knowledge in an unexpected capacity: as a social media strategist.

In their various careers, these linguists expressed a commitment to teaching through working with organizations that support teachers, or organizations that are about teaching, through managing and mentoring, instructional design, and coaching roles—and so we did actually touch on Business, Innovation, Technology, and Nonprofit in the discussion. Also, there were stories about some of the other professional capacities cultivated by academic study, namely editing and writing (as explored in the story of former professor Linda Lombardi) and project management (from Hillah, who works in software development for a financial firm). But what is NOT there ends up being in hindsight rather conspicuously loud. The "noisy not"—recalling our discussion of Charlotte Linde's attention to what's conspicuously absent—was that there weren't many stories specifically about research or the research sector.

In this book, I seek to balance that with a complement of stories of linguists working as researchers. I began this course correction in Chapter 1, with a peek at both Charlotte Linde and Anne Charity Hudley's formidable research careers, and in Chapter 2, many of the ten from BRIGHTEN did work in research. In this chapter, I explore careers in research by sharing a handful of stories from folks working in the areas of user research, taxonomy, and conversation design (AI and chatbots). To help me tell their stories, I will draw from some of the different kinds of storytelling genres we are called upon to use in talking about our work, including LinkedIn posts and profiles, professional portfolios, podcasts, and websites. In exploring these, I call attention to the ways that linguists' "ways of seeing" are on display in their ways of working. In each story I focus on one specific aspect of their work that I see as illuminating some of the ways of thinking and doing cultivated by training in linguistics and which now show up in how they approach their work, what Charles Goodwin calls "professional vision."

As with all the stories in this book, my hope is that seeing familiar aspects of linguistic study displayed in the work stories of others will help readers become more aware of the transferability of the skills and training of linguists. And especially for these areas of work that seem to be receiving a great deal of attention lately as places where linguistic analytical skills are particularly valued like user research, I hope some of the details herein contained might serve to spark some professional imaginations.

We'll start with user experience research and with someone just starting out in this world of work—Didem Ikizoğlu.

When I first started learning about the professional world of user research, one of the things that struck me was the importance of having a professional portfolio. I think I can date this realization to a meeting of the Bay Area Computer-Human Interaction meet-up (BayCHI), focused on the topic of professional portfolio development. At that meeting, I also had a long conversation with Janneke Van Hofwegen—who we will talk to later in this chapter—who at that time had just recently graduated with her PhD and was herself immersed in the process of presenting herself professionally and grappling with the task of assembling a portfolio. Having grasped over the course of that evening both the enormity and importance of the thing, I decided that the best way to explore what a portfolio is and does would be to do some user research myself. So I reached out to someone interested in the field, but not yet familiar with the genre and how it is used. I asked her if she would look at a portfolio along with me, talking aloud with me about what she saw as we thought our way through it.

Didem Ikizoğlu

Let's Get Meta!

So it was that I sat down to look at Abby Bajuniemi's excellent online portfolio with Didem Ikizoğlu, a linguistics graduate student who was at the time we sat down gearing up to defend her dissertation. In order to be ready to hit the ground running when she finished, Didem had been doing a bit of career exploration and education in the months leading up to her graduation—and just a quick note about that strategy: doing a bit of slow but steady career development in the background while focused on another major project. I know that I was very "all or nothing" when it came to thinking about career when I was a student, which is to say that I thought I would just "figure it out" somehow when I graduated. The career development literature suggests that searching for a job should be your full-time job. Such that if you are working on a dissertation, the only way forward would seem to be that you should focus sequentially (dissertation now, job search later), because you can't have two full-time jobs. But there are a few problems with this strategy, including that the job search takes time before it starts yielding results. Further, it is extremely emotionally difficult to be focused on job searching full-time, and it's also particularly punishing to start from scratch. Starting small and starting early addresses both.

And so Didem and I sat down over Zoom and looked at Abby's portfolio together using screenshare. I asked Didem to verbalize her thought process as she clicked through, and I asked questions like what was most calling her attention, what was confusing, what she had been expecting to see, etc. Not only did this enable her to learn a bit about the kinds of methods used by user researchers, she also got to see how these get talked about in a portfolio. All this, and she was able to experience a user interview—from the perspective of the user—at the same time. We started on the landing page—I have included a screenshot for reference (Figure 3.1).

Now, about Abby for a moment—she's a researcher, interaction designer, strategist, author, and speaker. Abby spoke to me a while back as part of my campfire series (on the Career Linguist YouTube channel), where she shared how she got started as a user researcher, and why she found it to be such a good fit, naming the intellectual stimulation as particularly satisfying.

Abby shared that she often gets asked, "You have a degree in Spanish Applied Linguistics? What does that have to do with user

FIGURE 3.1 *Landing page of Abby Bajuniemi's User Research portfolio*

experience or human factors?" She answers that the first and most obvious thing is that the research methods are pretty much one to one. People in the field will use card sorts, semanticists will use card sorts. If you are a user researcher thinking about information architecture—how to organize content on a web page, for example— you are going to be asking questions that any linguist will be familiar with, like: "How do I categorize different bits of language?" and "How do you go from high level to granular?" She gave the analogy to how linguists think about a language in its socio-political and historical and geographical context, for example, how in Caribbean Spanish we might see variation in question structure because of English language contact: "que tu quieres" or "que quieres tu?" Or that we can get really granular like: in one specific context of coda position in front of [a], an [s] will tend to be aspirated or alighted, but there's more retention in other contexts. Abby sees a direct connection from this research to how she thinks about information architecture.

I noted the connection to localization work, and Abby said that this is also something that she has done, where she's asking questions about "Who is your audience? Are they bilingual? Are they monolingual? What variety of Spanish do they speak?" Her training has enabled her to know how to properly translate content so it makes sense for a particular audience. She mentioned a recent example of a project where she was creating content for bilingual Spanish English teachers and needed to translate "close reading" or "textual analysis." In talking with the client, they shared that they anticipated having people with varying levels of proficiency or competence in either language. And so, she knew that she wanted to use words that weren't going to be only comprehensible to monolingual Spanish speakers, because in border states, sometimes there are a lot of calques, or borrowings, and it might actually be more appropriate to use some of those borrowed words. She continued, "It'll be okay to use some of the jargon in English, because that's probably how they're going to be using it, they're probably not going to be using the same terminology that a monolingual Spanish speaker in like Argentina, or whatever would use." Illuminating some of the considerations that Abby keeps in mind when she's doing localization work, I hope to spark a connection for some of you readers and illuminate some applications of your interests, skills, and training that you might not currently be thinking about.

So back now to me and Didem looking at Abby's portfolio. Didem lives in Seattle and has friends and family who work in tech—user researchers among them—so she did bring some expectations about what she would find in a portfolio. This meant that my ears really perked up when I first heard an expression of surprise from her, "She's laying out her whole methodology here!" which struck Didem so much that it led her to wonder whether this website was in fact deigned as training material instead of a portfolio.

Describe, Interpret, Evaluate (D.I.E. Rubric)

This moment of surprise is worth paying attention to—it's the kind of paying attention we cultivated when I taught the ethnography of communication course when students would use the *Describe, Interpret, Evaluate* rubric (unfortunate acronym D.I.E.) to slow down the meaning-making process so as to better see it unfolding. Didem's exclamation caught my attention because it signaled an evaluation, based on her interpretation of all this descriptive detail she observed. Often, our sense-making and meaning-making processes unfold so quickly, we jump straight over the first level—describing—so much so as to almost invisibilize it, and we fly over interpretation, not realizing that we choose one among many interpretations, to arrive at an evaluation: "this seems wrong!" But we—all of us—can remind ourselves to peel back to "description" because it is the foundation of the process and where we can really sink in our teeth as analysts.

So, I asked Didem if she knew where her expectations about detail might be coming from. What was she comparing this portfolio to in order to observe a level of detail that would strike her so powerfully so as to make her doubt the genre. She guessed that perhaps she was comparing to a LinkedIn page. I shared that seeing sections like "Method" and "Results" had led me initially to think that portfolios were more like academic research papers. Didem echoed that this was what might have contributed to the "transparency" that she was noticing. "Transparency," another evaluation that served to remind us to probe back for observable, linguistic features that we might describe. Didem put her finger on an example describing the number of rounds of observations and for how many minutes they lasted. Now with something describe-able, we have something that we can analyze: How does descriptive detail (i.e., rounds of observations) mean differently in different contexts?

For example, when it comes to crafting academic writing, we assume that the audience are other researchers, and we share methodological detail so that our research can be replicated. Such a move is likely to be interpreted as being collegial, helpful (didactic even, hence Didem's sense of familiarity to training genres) in the academic context. But if we're thinking about LinkedIn, it's harder to know who the reader might be, and there may be a need to be more protective as reflected in the conversational move that followed Didem's expression of surprise: she moved into concern that giving so much detail would leave the researcher open to having their ideas taken and her labor stolen. But the portfolio genre is neither academic research paper nor LinkedIn. It is designed to be read by a prospective employer and as such the level of descriptive detail about methodology is a demonstration of mastery and experience with research design and project management to encourage someone to appreciate the researcher's ability to thoughtfully design a scope of work. It demonstrates that she will be able to make appropriate estimation of time and budget, while at the same time being adaptable and flexible when the situation calls for it.

Now, in telling this story here, I have used the D.I.E. rubric to describe my ways of paying attention (to Didem's ways of paying attention) because I want you the reader to be paying attention to your paying attention in the same way. When you hear something that "sparks" with you—something concrete and observable—I want to ask you to see how you might interpret and evaluate. This might be in the stories you notice others telling about how you work or the stories they tell about how they work. Listen for things that exemplify how you think and frame problems, how you choose to approach and address them (and consider how they may have been shaped by your training in linguistics). I also call attention to D.I.E. as a way to slow down the meaning-making process because I want to cultivate your awareness about your own interpretive meaning-making in real time. This skill is valuable in any context, but especially so in work. In thinking about work, it behooves us to become more aware of multiple options (ways of seeing things, and ways of moving forward). When we take the time to *Describe*, *Interpret*, and *Evaluate*, we know something more about what we are choosing and why.

This is important in job-seeking interactions especially, where the stakes can be particularly high. My training in linguistics helped me to cue into the linguistic feature that jumped out at Didem (descriptive detail about methodology) in making sense of Abby's portfolio, because it was the very same evaluative reaction that I had to the very same feature in a related genre—a job ad—from this same world of work, user research.

The job advertisement asked for:

- Experience designing and conducting user research using a variety of methodologies.

- Experience recruiting and scheduling participants (customers and prospects).

- A proven track record of working well with developers, product managers, designers and business partners.

- Ability to use inferential as well as descriptive statistics and identify the right sample size for a given project.

This would-be employer asks that a candidate be able to "identify the right sample size for a given project" and to demonstrate "experience recruiting and scheduling participants." Detailed description of methodological design turns out to be precisely the kind of information that an employer seems to use in order to be able to make a hiring decision! And yet, when I first saw this ad, I'll share that I felt intense resistance. I think I emailed it to a friend who works in user research to ask if this was "normal." Describing it to you now, I can tell you that I vaulted straight over *Describe* moving quickly through *Interpret*—"They think I don't know how to do this!"—and landing squarely in *Evaluation*, reacting with righteous indignation ("OF COURSE I know how to decide the right sample size for a project," "Who do you think you are dealing with?"), which—I'll be honest—led me to set aside that job application and never apply. At that time, I didn't acknowledge what might be fueling this reaction.

Your reactions may well be different, but I share this example as an invitation to pay attention to your own moments of evaluation, especially if you find yourself experiencing something of the "whaaaat?!?!" variety during a job interview or other high-stakes job-seeking context. In my case, I found that I needed to do some "human homework"—as my friend Beth Duckles from the Open Post Academics networking group calls it—to work through some unacknowledged grief around the twin losses of the academic professional path and academic community. I needed to acknowledge and work through some of the assumptions about how to talk about research that I had cultivated while working as an academic. When you are an academic, surrounded by academics, everyone knows what you are talking about, because you are surrounded by people who were similarly trained. I needed to work through some of these feelings of loss before I could move forward. If possible, it's good to work through these feelings now so that they don't get in the way of being present to learning more about a job opportunity that might be a good fit.

I have found the B.A.R. response as described by author Maura Cullen in her book *35 Dumb Things that Well-Intentioned People Say* to be another useful strategy. In this case, it helps me to actually do D.I.E. in the moment. B.A.R. stands for "breathe, acknowledge, and respond." B.A.R. slows things down to buy a bit of time. When you can recognize that there has been an evaluation, you can go back to the descriptive level so that you can know what you're actually dealing with. D.I.E. is probably one of the most powerful analytical tools I learned as a researcher. It's just one example of how we can be linguists for ourselves to be better linguists for the world.

So we return once again to the user interview with Didem, for just some last descriptive observations about Abby's portfolio to close out our discussion. The image and label that most looked to Didem like what she had been expecting to find in a portfolio was one that described work that Abby had done for a restaurant—Brassa Rotisserie. This research project involved studying the implementation of, employee engagement with, and execution of an open-book management system (a way of giving employees access to and a sense of ownership of financial and organizational information). As part of her research, Abby looked at the role of language in this implementation, given that the majority of the employees were Spanish-speaking and the system (and management) used English.

Didem started to imagine herself doing a study like this one, with a local community organization that she is currently involved with, which I found particularly gratifying because when I had first looked at Abby's portfolio, I had had the exact same thought. If you are thinking of looking into user research, do a project with an organization that you are already involved with and care about. This would not only be learning experience, it would give you a portfolio piece, and be network- and community-building, and in talking about it, your enthusiasm would likely naturally come through.

Abby's restaurant project was also a great one to explore with Didem (and useful for sharing here) because it involved the use of many different methods from the User Experience toolkit: interviews and surveys, experience map and flow chart, facilitated group discussion, curriculum development, and personas. Because the idea of personas as a research tool was new to her, Didem and I ended up spending a large part of our conversation talking about their use and value.

For readers in the same situation, I'll quickly share some thinking about personas from the Nielson Norman Group (NNG), a great resource for information about all things user experience research (the organizational web page for IDEO is another). NNG's 2015 article "Personas Make Users Memorable for Product Team Members" reminds that "the field of user experience centers on the idea that we must design products around people, rather than teaching people how to use products: user-centered design (UCD), not technology-centered design. In order to do so, we must understand people—their behaviors, attitudes, needs, and goals." Personas are fictional constructions, characters who are designed to be detailed and realistic archetypes that can help various members of the team practice empathetically keeping the user's needs, concerns, and goals in mind.

The first handful of articles about personas that I came across on the NNG website reflect critical engagement with the ultimate purpose and utility and need for improvement of this method, likely to be true for any central method (focus groups, interviews, and surveys). Researchers will likely be called upon to show both technical mastery as well as display some critical distance toward personas and other tools, indicating awareness of what the tool is good for, and what it is not best used for. In short, a researcher would likely need to demonstrate that she does not use any tool blindly or naïvely.

From the 2018 piece "Why Personas Fail," a caution: these "human-like snapshots of relevant and meaningful commonalities in your customer groups" can get misunderstood and misused. As with any method, tool, or technique—it is good for the researcher to have many tools at her disposal and not to be overly attached to any particular one. Like an artist, displaying mastery and expertise means holding tools lightly.

So now let's turn to stories from four such research artists: Greg Bennett, who works at Salesforce on the Einstein Bots team; Janneke Van Hofwegen, who works as a User Experience Researcher at a large tech company in Silicon Valley; Eli Asikin-Garmager, a user researcher at the Wikimedia Foundation; and Anthony Koch, a taxonomist at the job search site Indeed.

Let's start with Greg.

And more precisely—keeping things a little bit meta—we'll talk to Greg's colleague Molly about what it's like to work with Greg!

Greg Bennet

Talking about Talk

"Adjacency Pairs!" was Molly's enthusiastic response when I sat down to talk with her at Salesforce Tower about what it's like to work with linguist Greg Bennet. "He taught us about adjacency pairs, and it is just so wonderful to learn about something that is absolutely essential to our work that none of us would have ever known about!" At Salesforce, Greg works on a team called Einstein Bots—researching ways of making conversations with chatbots go more smoothly, or as Greg puts it, "Taking what we know about conversations and bringing them over to bots."

I went to Salesforce to be able to hear from Molly about working with Greg because this book itself is designed to help readers gain a bit of perspective on their own experience. Why not directly ask your current and former colleagues and collaborators: "Can you think of any examples from working with me that demonstrate how I think about language and communication?"

Molly observed how effortlessly Greg manages outreach. He gives lots of talks, but this did not happen on its own. He has consistently advocated for speaking opportunities, from Molly's perspective, seemingly informed by a conviction that taking the time to talk about work is worthwhile. By bringing others along into your ways of seeing and thinking, you build a community of collaborators and potential advocates. At the same time, Molly also observed that Greg seems to have an intuition about when to—and when not to—push his case, say at a team meeting, or when "socializing" research insights. A commitment to communication that acknowledges the challenge but perceives the worth of both time and effort.

So let's look at a couple examples of his talk about work. We'll start by thinking about LinkedIn posts. Here's one that he posted about a conference presentation (Figure 3.2).

By posting regularly what he is working on and thinking about, Greg demonstrates HOW he works, details about the day-to-day. For the people with whom he directly works, it keeps them thinking about how to support him in the process of job crafting: keeping an eye out for challenges that his linguistic skills will enable him to be uniquely equipped to solve. For others in the community who are not as familiar with User Experience, his updates give insight and inspiration—to know more about what the work entails so as to decide whether or not they might want to do it/might need to hire someone to do it.

In another post, he shared that he had just been interviewed for a podcast (Figure 3.3).

In this podcast interview, Greg introduces his academic training in sociolinguistics as I have often heard him do—by sharing a story about an IM chat that got him interested in what John Gumperz calls Contextualization Cues. You can practically hear his interviewer lean in as he describes the role that conversational style played in his first major heartbreak:

I was chatting with this guy and I got dumped over IM chat
And I could feel it coming!

I kinda remember thinking to myself at the time

"how is it that I can feel someone being distant or distancing themselves from me?

Or being cold,

when I can't hear his voice, see his face, um you know gestures, any of that."

normally we get that through conversation

you know face to face

or even through intonation over the phone

and you know, as one is very wont to do after one's first major heartbreak,

I was like "I have to figure out what happened, and unpack it!"

And so, I took a class

It was interesting because I was just signing up for classes

I think for the Fall semester

And they offered a class called Text and Talk

Which was an introductory course for graduate students

To the field of conversation and discourse analysis

So analyzing using linguistics structures and patterns of conversation

And that was really my foray into using linguistics to look at online chat practices.

Working as a conversation designer, Greg's research into how people communicate things like emotion, tone, and personality through text uniquely prepares him to be equipped to think about how text can convey personality. He can help his team be able to design tools that would help the bot come across as being more happy-go-lucky, or more involved, or serious, or, or, or.

I call little stories like Greg's, about how a text breakup fueled his research interest, "pocket examples," and I advocate having them at the ready to be able to quickly engage your listener into understanding something important about how you work. In this case, it is how academic training in sociolinguistics is relevant to the world of conversation design. As implied by the name "pocket example," it's a good idea to have a small set (a pocket full) of them at the ready. The activity at the end of this chapter will show you how.

Greg Bennett · 1st ...
Conversation Design Lead at Salesforce
1yr · 🌐

When worlds collide: Dragonball Z meets #EinsteinBots meets #linguistics on stage at #TrailheaDX19. I have to pinch myself in moments like these—I never once thought as a grad student in sociolinguistics years ago that I'd end up working for an organization that actively seeks and *celebrates* my take on how linguistics can make or break a customer's experience of a #chatbot (with a bit of my childhood cartoon fandom mixed in)!

Many thanks to:

- George Hu for being an amazing co-pilot;

- Noel Lamb for guiding us on our journey to the stage and for taking these excellent photos that make me look way cooler than I am in real life;

- the fantastic audience of Salesforce admins, developers, partners, customers, and fellow coworkers for being open to this research (and cheering extra hard for DBZ);

- and especially Salesforce UX for empowering me to bring my whole self to my work.

To view the talk recording, visit the "Resources" section at https://lnkd.in /gM7zdYY. #TDX19

FIGURE 3.2 *Greg Bennett LinkedIn post about a conference presentation*

Greg Bennett · 1st
Conversation Design Lead at Salesforce
2mo · 🌐   • • •

I had a blast talking #ConversationDesign, #linguistics, and #UX with Botsociety on their podcast! Check out the recording: https://lnkd.in /gxJxW5R.

#userexperience #chatbots #voice #VUI #userresearch

Botsociety
2,097 followers   + Follow
2mo · Edited · 🌐

🔥 The #ConversationDesign #Podcast Episode 6 is out now!

Greg Bennett, Conversation Design Lead at Salesforce shared with us some really cool thoughts, such as the importance of conducting UX research when building a chatbot.
According to Greg, when it comes to conversation design, we all have assumptions about how the conversation should go and they are based on our personal experience and cultural background. In fact, every community has its own conversational style and they might be quite different.
In order to unpack our assumptions, we have to do UX research and conduct usability testing or concept evaluation on the conversation design.

🎧 Find it wherever you listen to your podcast or click on the link in comments!

Greg Bennett on Applying Linguistics to Conversation Design

𝒞 Botsociety
Conversation Design Podcast

🔥 💙 💚 47 · 2 Comments

FIGURE 3.3 *Greg Bennett LinkedIn post about a podcast*

Staying with LinkedIn for a moment, let's switch over to a profile, one of another sociolinguist—Janneke Van Hofwegen. Since this was the profile that she used to get the job—her first in user research—I'll tell her story as she talks about herself in her LinkedIn summary. Put yourself into the perspective of her prospective employer as we make our way through, and you'll perhaps see how her ways of talking about herself engender a sense of trust.

Janneke Van Hofwegen

Telling Her Story through Her LinkedIn Summary

As a User Experience Researcher, Janneke spends her days talking to people about booking travel: those who are looking to book hotels and hotel owners and staff (ranging from small, independent hoteliers up to those who work for the big chains) who are seeking to host. We'll hear more about a former linguistics professor turned independent hotelier in Chapter 5, but for Janneke, she's accumulating and organizing information to share with developers about the kinds of user, the things that they care about, what they are looking for, and where and how they are looking for it. She thinks with would-be guests about what would help them make a decision to purchase a hotel stay, and what will make them feel most comfortable doing so through her organization's travel products.

I confess that I hadn't really thought about hotels like a researcher before, but after only just a few minutes of talking with Janneke, I started realizing that the whole experience is very tied up in the construction and performance of identity. First off, there's all of the ways that we travel: for work or for adventure, or for relaxation, or for family—we kind of want the place we're staying to feel like it "fits." But really, there are so many different goals: wanting to experience local culture or seeing everything there is to see, or needing to get away from it all, rest and recoup, or blow off some steam. So many factors that would shape what we would be looking for in making a purchasing decision. Hotels need to think about how to convey lots of information pretty quickly (since most people probably don't want to spend that much time on this decision either). So yeah, her job has plenty of meaty questions about language, culture, and identity!

Here's how she described herself in the first paragraph of her LinkedIn summary:

> As a researcher, I focus on understanding human behavior and stylistic expression through the lens of language and group/ individual identity. I want to know what matters to people in order to facilitate the production of tools and applications that will truly impact and enrich their lives. My educational background and research experience ensure that I can bring rich, creative insight about people's needs and experiences and produce actionable results for companies to use in product development.

Notice how she frames her foci and research interests in terms of what these enable her to be able to do for an organization—using phrases such as "in order to" to help a reader know what to expect in terms of outcomes of her analytical abilities. She describes "produc[ing] actionable results for companies to use in product development" and "facilitat[ing] the production of tools and applications that will truly impact and enrich their lives," a discursive move that we might have called a "because of that" in my improv days. It is of a kind with the shifts that we will explore through an activity in Chapter 5 when we consider where to place the narrative focus when we tell stories about our work (hint: it's about Results!).

As people who value learning things, we often subconsciously spend much time and devote our narrative attention describing internal states, things that piqued our interest—something we noticed, what we thought about it, how it felt inside, in our minds. However, such description is not ideal if we want to help someone see how we work. To show how we work is to shift forward to bring narrative focus to showing what happened as a result of that realization. Janneke is interested in human behavior and stylistic expression, and she focuses on language as a means of expressing group/individual identity, which helps her understand what matters to people. But it is her "and because of that ... " that really makes this powerful to a reader who might want to hire her. Because of the focus and understanding, she is able to facilitate the production of impactful tools and applications.

Janneke told me that one of the things that makes her very good at her job is her ability to cultivate trust, something she practiced and cultivated over the course of her academic research work as a sociolinguist. In conducting on-site ethnographic fieldwork, it's important to be able to listen, pay careful attention to how others are behaving, and know how it is that you are being received. Notice how Janneke describes this aspect of her background in the next section of her LinkedIn summary:

> I have deep experience in qualitative research: ethnographic observation and interviewing, diary studies, focus groups. I've also designed and administered surveys and conducted lab experiments. My additional background in quantitative methods means I am the whole package—I manage complex projects from inception to completion, comfortable with all phases of the research process.

There are a few things to notice here about how she describes methodologies and methodological frameworks. For one thing, she highlights specific approaches and methods that she is experienced in using, helping the reader organize them as either qualitative or quantitative, and just generally giving more description that she likely would have done in another genre like an academic CV. Further, she then puts these into the context of a larger project, describing how she manages research in business terms. A dissertation is really about project management: "manage complex projects from inception to completion, comfortable with all phases of the research process." Having conducted independent research projects like theses or dissertations really tells an employer that someone with a PhD knows how to shepherd people and processes along under complex, ambiguous, and ever-changing conditions and often with competing objectives and timelines. And for someone to have successfully submitted and defended the thing, they showed an ability to manage projects and products with the end result in mind.

Finally, in her third and final paragraph, Janneke talks about something else that many of us who are emerging from being a student don't tend to think about: our management experience.

I am also a seasoned manager: I can lead teams for both small—and large-scale program and project management endeavors. I am a natural-born collaborator and am driven toward achievable outcomes and efficiency—elements integral to my success in managing many scholarly and practical projects. My broad publication record illustrates my commitment to producing specific, detailed, and measurable outcomes and my ability to communicate them to a broad audience.

With the above three sections, Janneke adheres to an oft-seen pattern for describing oneself in a LinkedIn summary. In this case, it is three different aspects of her experience as a researcher: starting with what she does (and why); moving on to how she does it; and ending with, "with/for whom," describing how she relates to colleagues and research stakeholders (in this case, those who read her publications).

Her ending place is a great place to begin for those who are just starting to practice talking about academic experience to nonacademics. In an academic context, publications can be left to "speak for themselves" more or less. On a CV, for example, one can simply mention that one was published in X, Y, or Z journal and can safely assume that those in the field will know everything that entails. For someone who isn't familiar with the rigor that XYZ journal is known for, and who hasn't necessarily been through the peer-review process, the significance and relevance must be interpreted, unpacked, and explained. Janneke helps by describing her publication record as "broad" and as demonstrating her commitment to precision in her work and again to breadth when it comes to disseminating her findings. The adjectives she uses capture the nature of research findings that a prospective employer is likely to look for in a candidate: specific, detailed, and measurable.

Bringing the focus to describing her research outcomes (the deliverables) rather than the process is part of the audience design work that an academic must do when communicating about research with nonacademics.

Let's turn now to another linguist/user researcher: Eli Asikin-Garmager.

Eli Asikin-Garmager

Designing Collaboration

At the Wikimedia Foundation, linguist Dr. Eli Asikin-Garmager is a design researcher on the languages team. One of their areas of focus is the content translation product (teams and work in the UX world tend to be organized around a product), a tool that helps with the translation of Wikipedia articles. Now, given the way that Wikipedia operates, people who doing the work of translation are likely not professional translators, which presents some interesting challenges for a User Experience Researcher. For folks not familiar with the organization—or who haven't really given much thought to the behind-the-scenes of how the work life of the Wikimedia Foundation's staff might be organized—let's first take a step back.

The Wikimedia Foundation is a nonprofit organization founded in 2003 by Jimmy Wales as a way to fund his Wikipedia project along with ten other wikis that follow the free content model. As part of the Open Movement, their main goal is the dissemination of knowledge, and although there are 300 employees at the foundation, the vast majority of the work of creating articles is done by thousands and thousands of volunteer editors. According to a recent profile piece in *Wired* (titled "Wikipedia is the Last Best Place on the Internet"), it's much more than an encyclopedia: "Wikipedia has become a community, a library, a constitution, an experiment, a political manifesto—the closest thing there is to an online public square." Richard Cooke, the author of this piece, credits its "not to be underestimated" emotional architecture: "Wikipedia is built on the personal interests and idiosyncrasies of its contributors; in fact, without getting gooey, you could even say it is built on love."

In my conversation with Eli, what came across to me most most powerfully was an experience of a collaborative and carefully considered workplace culture, a highly democratized approach to research, and a sense of real shared ownership of the work. He described gatherings like design reviews and research share-outs where standard operating procedure is for as many stakeholders as possible—people invested in the outcome of the work—to show up, which diversity of thought of course makes the work better. As the name might suggest, working on the languages team is highly international and intercultural competence is important and highly valued. Core members of the team are in India, Israel, Spain, Finland, Greece, and San Francisco (Eli lives in the Midwest; he works remotely). As a linguist, he feels like what he brings is a "general sensitivity to the atoms of language." But more than that, he has found his background as a UX writer to be useful in the task of communicating about workflow with colleagues. He shared a general strategic approach that he had developed at the request of a former boss at a former financial technology company, who suggested that it might be helpful to visualize "what we know" and "how we learn" on an *x/y* axis.

Here's the result (Figure 3.4).

Eli thanks the members of his team for conversations and feedback that informed his thinking on this schematic, which reveals some of the processes and decisions that structure work so as to enable groups to collaborate on conceptualizing a research plan. Although,

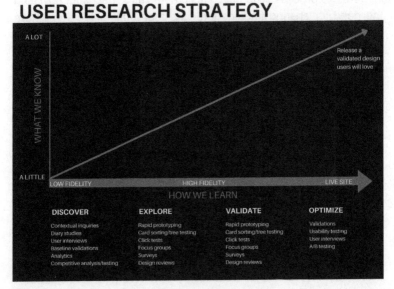

FIGURE 3.4 *Eli Asikin-Garmager schematic: What we know and how we learn*

he notes that the work specifics, including methods and how they group, are likely to vary across contexts (team, company, region, sector, etc.).

What struck me was how inviting this all feels—and how it reflects not only an inclination and willingness, but a specific strategy—for engaging colleagues from different functional orientations into the research early and often in the research and design process. After moving to the Bay Area, I started attending user research meetups and networking events to learn more about this world of work, and a phrase that jumped out at me from these circles is talk of "evangelizing" findings or "socializing" them. Granted, I am an outsider, but it is likely precisely this outsider perspective that made this word "ping" on my radar as a way of conceptualizing the process of communicating with colleagues because it presupposes distance, ignorance, and perhaps even resistance. The evangelism frame brings with it (for me at least) differentials along the axes of power and knowledge, where the person with the power and information does the evangelizing, and it feels rather one-way. A "noisy not" from my conversation with Eli was the absence of the evangelism frame; indeed, this process schematic was created as a means for obviating the need for sharing findings after the fact: stakeholders will have been along for the ride. Given what I learned from speaking to Eli about Wikipedia's culture, I am not surprised to see that even this— perhaps especially this—aspect of research is different at Wikipedia. Collaboration is the name of the game.

But what do the languages team actually DO, you ask? Well, they help with the task of translation. They work on designing a product that matches the natural workflow of those who are participating in the day-to-day work of translating articles. A big part of this work involves something that they call "validating interactions" or simply validating, which involves identifying assumptions about how the tool will be used, and then checking those out, or validating them. As Eli explained, validation involves actively confirming that something is working well, and not simply being content because you have not observed problems. There could be things that are important to know that are simply not visible. In the case of the translation tool, designers might be making assumptions about the workflow, which get built into their design brought over from how professional interpretation work is structured, including that translation might proceed sentence by sentence or that an editor would tackle an article at a time. While in actuality, for many of the editors, it is more likely that someone would be working on a chunk of an article while they're waiting for a bus (thus, more likely to be using their cellphone rather than a computer). So, Eli's team has implemented a workflow derived from their User Experience Research about how multilingual people actually translate and interact with their technology and with Wikipedia.

All of which is to say that successful validation all comes down to researchers and designers being able to carve out meaningful units of analysis, which again is a collaborative process, actively informed by the user research process itself.

For formally trained linguists who excel at writing and might be interested in breaking into the world of User Experience Research, Eli suggests looking into UX writing, and he shared a couple resources, which I share in the Reference section at the end of the book.[1]

The final story for this chapter comes from Anthony Koth, who works as a taxonomist.

Anthony Koth

Taxonomists Define the World

At the beginning of our conversation, Anthony Koth reminded me of something that I had forgotten that I had learned: Categorization Theory. He used an example that I must have done as part of my own coursework in semantics, it rang so familiar to me (Stallion = Horse + Male). This classical approach to biological taxonomy from semantics is a pocket example that Anthony shares to explain how he fulfills the "we help people get jobs" tagline of Indeed as part of his work at that company.

He works as a taxonomist.

"Essentially," as he puts it, "the job is discourse analysis of job ads and resumes."

According to Anthony, a person who will be highly successful as a taxonomist would be highly collaborative and good at coordinating and communicating. And, for those who might be more research-inclined, there are other departments that run focus panels like diary studies, or ethnographies, with job seekers and with employers trying to see how their products are or aren't matching up with expectations to improve the usability of the product.

At Indeed, they use different taxonomies, each with different types of data and with varying degrees of precision and recall to make sure they get enough in each group and that it's good data. Anthony and his fellow taxonomists—many of whom are trained in library science—figure out ways to organize "all of these data points into useful packages that the engineers can then take and work with the buckets and bins we put the job ads into." They also help tune the search algorithm, so that if someone goes to the website and searches for something like "consultant" (a notoriously difficult term to categorize), the searcher gets something close in the industry they are trying to get into. In trying to refine their taxonomies, they look outside of Indeed to consider external job taxonomies—like the one put out by the Bureau of Labor Statistics, to derive and develop tools that work. Keywords used to describe the work of a taxonomist might include ontology, knowledge management, taxonomy governance, and management, often with connections to work in labeling, meta-data, and machine learning.

Anthony just recently graduated with his PhD with a focus on Semantics and Cognitive Linguistics. Since he is so close to the process—just months out—I'll share the navigation part of the story in his voice:

> After I finished, I started having to figure out "okay, I need this job thing." And I kind of knew early on that academia was not going to be my career because of various things that happened to me as a student and seeing and hearing the state of academia. I had a couple friends working in academia in different respects, and it just never seemed like my world. So, as I was trying to get around to finding a job, I considered various options. I was looking at government contracting work. I was looking at digital humanities. For example, at Virginia Tech in their digital humanities library section they needed a combination of Computer Management and technical skills plus laboratory teaching for things like data mining and text analytics; things that I used in my dissertation process.

So that would have been kind of fun, because I would have been in education but not necessarily in "publish or perish."

I also looked back to where I had been in life and the other jobs I'd had, to see if maybe it was worth returning to a previous career, because grad school can be kind of a mid-career break, if you will. So, I started looking at theater work again, but I also wound up talking to a friend who's at Adobe, who works in UX (user experience), knowledge management and design. He gave me some keywords and terms and then from there, I got to taxonomy. I had not thought about that at all as something that is actively done. I started looking for some taxonomy positions and ultimately ended up at Indeed.

One of the reasons Anthony is so happy at Indeed is that they seem open to hearing about how linguists might help them refine their processes, and he's currently working on bringing more current semantic analyses into his work—for example, exemplar clouds. His managers have given time that he can set aside to work on this "pet project," and he is excited about this opportunity to craft his job (as we discussed in Chapter 2). Anthony hopes that bringing clustering analysis—a more rigorous and mathematically backed approach—might show how a given taxonomy agrees with variation and change from industry to industry and position to position. He's hoping for an "ah-ha" moment.

I asked him if he could walk us through a typical day.

Work tasks typically come as a "ticket" through the ticketing system, JIRA. These tickets report a problem or an issue to address in the taxonomy, such as rules that label data. For example, if the rules are written too broadly, there could be a batch of job ads in Node X (catching too high in the taxonomy), which they call "bloat." So Anthony will work to refine the rules to move things down the nodes so that the job ad is where it's supposed to be in the taxonomy, and a user search yields a more manageable result.

As he explains, there are some job titles, such as *project manager*, that can be problematic for a taxonomy because it can be in so many different types of industries and fields, it winds up in a couple places in the taxonomy. You can be a project manager in architecture, or you can be a project manager in health services, and while there are meaningful ways that the work would be similar, there are also important ways that the work would be different, both things that you would want to capture in your taxonomy.

Another example project might involve looking at keywords, trying to figure out how to isolate them in different systems, and see whether the taxonomists might figure out a way to bring some more automaticity to the process. So that's just raw data coding. An example of that might be making tags like *green jobs* or *veteran-owned* or *minority-owned* businesses. Such suggestions come from within the taxonomy department and from other stakeholders to make the platform more usable, the data more searchable.

Sometimes he gets to research things like how work gets organized in a particular sector. Based on what he learns, he can better parse out the jobs within that industry to get more clarity and specificity to work through categorizing some of the more ambiguous job ads or titles.

And then of course there's Zoom meetings. Lots and lots of Zoom meetings.

To close out our conversation, I asked Anthony what he would say to someone who might be interested in pursuing taxonomy. He started by sharing some search terms: *information architecture, knowledge management, knowledge curation, content management.* He also shared that in the job ads for taxonomists, you'll see that they're generally looking for people with a library sciences degree. "Because the idea is you're organizing information, so you're building a system, a classification system, and then you're figuring out ways to make sure things are classified correctly." But this does not mean that linguists need not apply!

As Anthony explained, what taxonomy—at least on the tech side—does is to append metadata to pieces of data, which have to be collected and organized. So a tag that tells you, "Okay, this is specifically a sales job or this is specifically a sports piece or this is specifically a political piece. Is it political opinion, political fact, future planning? What aspect under political is economics versus health policy?" Basically, taxonomists get the data from everyone, and then they create a unified vocabulary. You can see why librarians tend to have that skill set and why these kinds of jobs came out of library science. But, if you've done any kind of linguistic analysis, you've got the skill set. We're the pattern masters. We can work with any kind of data—that is a skill we have naturally learned.

As he says, "We have a proclivity for it—that's why we become linguists." But then we also learn all the tools to break things down into pieces and figure out, "Okay, does this type of definition scheme work? No. Okay, tweak it a little bit. Okay. This definition scheme seems to be better."

If you couldn't tell that Anthony loves his work, ask him what it means to say that taxonomists "define the world."

A Story from Me: The Work Interrogatives

I started my blog Career Linguist to get linguists to think more broadly and widely about career. Since its inception, at this point nearly ten years ago, the page that has been the most popular year after year has been "Fifty Organizations," a list of organizations that currently employ linguists. I update the list when a linguist reaches out to me to say "I love my job!"—and when that happens, I look at the list and remove an organization that I haven't heard about in a while or where my connection has left. Reflecting on the popularity of the page, I know that it is because this information is useful to jobseekers. But at the same time, it is likely the way the information is presented that is so attractive. People tend to be looking for a list.

And I am interested in engineering a mindset shift.

So I thought about what I really wanted my blog to do. What did I want people to come away with after looking at Career Linguist? Mainly, I wanted to get readers thinking in ways that were much more fine-grained than just "working as a linguist." I would hope they would start to think about the work sector more broadly and beyond their organization. And then ask, "Well, what does the person actually do at that organization? With whom and for whom? And why?" I started blogging about The Work Interrogatives—the WHO, WHAT, WHEN, WHERE, WHY, and HOW of work. Ultimately, I hope this line of questioning brings a sense of possibility and abundance.

As we discussed, BRIGHTEN was designed to expand the common understanding of the fields in which linguists (or indeed anyone) might work. But once we focus on a sector, we systems thinkers know that there is so much deeper we might then go. What organization? What role at that organization?

A Catalyst for You: Be a User Researcher for Yourself

Find a job ad (or if you're not in job search mode, the LinkedIn profile of a person whose work interests you), and pay attention for some aspect of their job that strikes you. Use the Work Interrogatives—the WHO, WHAT, WHEN, WHERE, WHY, and HOW—to begin reflecting. Maybe this could become the basis for some job crafting like we talked about in Chapter 2?

When it comes to job ads, there are three questions that are particularly important: WHAT (what are they asking you to do?); HOW (how do they want you to do it?); and WHY (why do they say it matters?). See Appendix 2 for a worksheet that will help you identify the big ideas that you need to address in your materials should you decide to apply for this job.

What Jumps Out?

Maybe it's a new concept, term, or idea. Maybe you can hear a bit of an "echo" or just some inclination that a concept gets used slightly differently than you tend to use it (I described something along these lines in the last chapter for the terms "technical assistance" and "development").

Listen, be curious, and look for ways to learn more, opportunities to ask questions.

And if you find yourself having a strong evaluative reaction, reflect—use B.A.R. (breathe, acknowledge, and respond) rather than R.A.B. (react, attack, and only then maybe perhaps decide to breathe) as described earlier in this chapter to get back to the beginning. Take the time to *Describe* that which is prompting *Interpretation* and informing your *Evaluation*.

4

Decide to BRIGHTEN Here and Now

Career advice is so often framed as help moving from a place of not knowing to one of knowing, but in my experience, this isn't the way that most people experience career. There is clarity in moments, but there is also plenty of productive disorientation. After all, if you are truly allowing yourself to be radically curious and explore, of course you will lose your bearings: you haven't been here before: no one has! We often cannot foresee how things will unfold, because opportunities reveal themselves when they reveal themselves.

In 2019, I had the opportunity to go to Finland to give career workshops at the University of Jyväskylä (JVU) as part of a collaboration with Robert Lawson, with whom I am developing teaching materials and pedagogical approaches to the application of language studies beyond academia. Rob was a visiting scholar at JVU that term, and I had so many great conversations with his colleagues and students over the course of that week, but was surprised (and perhaps not surprised at the same time) to hear from the graduate students that the thing they most wanted us to focus on in our discussions with them was imposter syndrome.

Recent research on imposter syndrome shared by cognitive psychologist Adam Grant in his book *Think Again* (2021) indicates that this feeling of being out of one's depth accompanies growth, which would explain why we see it so often with PhD students and others who are challenging and growing themselves. Further, this research indicates that it leads to better thinking because it fosters curiosity and reexamination. Other researchers have noted that because women and people of color experience the phenomenon more often, it is likely a result of experiencing bias, the manifestation of lingering conceptions about who belongs. These biases must be challenged, which takes work, and calls for allies. For those of you reading this book from a well-established position, or who belong to groups that have historically been centered in the workplace, perhaps this can serve as a catalyst to step forward and "call in" as Anne talked about in Chapter 1.

Back to Finland, I had not been exposed to the more recent thinking about imposter syndrome as a moment to call for allyship. So, what I shared with the Finnish grad students was a reframe: A campaign from Finnair that I had seen on my plane ride over about how *sometimes you have to travel to nowhere to be now here* (Figure 4.1).

FIGURE 4.1 *Now/Here campaign—Finnair. Designer: Antero Jokinen. The concept was developed for Finnair by Head of Finnair Holidays Kristiina Kukkohovi and Creative Directors Antero Jokinen and Iina Merikallio.*

Designer Antero Jokinen had playfully taken the words now and here and smushed them together to be now/here (nowhere) to connect that feeling of being lost with the concept of being somewhere so far away that you are able to be truly present to the now and here. Choosing to find happiness in productive disorientation struck me as a perfect way to embrace that feeling of being lost, which seems absolutely essential to career exploration and growth.

I also would argue that a contributing factor to the proliferation of the misconception that only we are lost (that everyone else has it all figured out) is owing to the fact that career stories don't tend to be shared when they are in the midst of their unfolding. We don't hear about other people's messy moments, so it seems abnormal to experience confusion, disorientation, or uncertainty. Rather than silencing such stories, I share many of them here, and hope you will invite, share, and discuss more of them in your own communities as part of your own career growth. Such stories contain wisdom about holding uncertainty and ambiguity and myriad potential possibilities. And in fact, to be very now/here about it, I'll share the story from me now and here (instead of at the end of the chapter as I have done in the other chapters!).

A Story from Me: Forensics Is Also about Poetry

I can remember sitting in my office just a few weeks into a one-year appointment at Howard University—an HBCU (Historically Black College or University) in Washington, DC—when there was a knock on the door. "My friend said that you are a linguist, and that you could help me with this piece I'm preparing for an upcoming forensics competition?" I was brand-new at the school, and a complete unknown to most everybody, but one of my students had apparently told her friend that I might be able to help. But I felt anxious—I was an adjunct and a linguist in an English Department at that. I knew that I probably wouldn't have the same approach to poetry or literary analysis that her English Department faculty would be using with her. Oh, and then I thought about performance! Who was her forensics coach? Was it someone in the Theater Department? I was at that time working on my dissertation on improvisational theatrical performance, which had me thinking—too much probably!—about performance theory, and I felt like I couldn't claim expertise.

I sat there awash in imposter syndrome. Perhaps sensing my ambivalence, she rushed in to clarify that while forensics is popularly associated with crime shows, the kind of forensics she was talking about had to do with verbal art, which I knew because I had done forensics in high school. We both laughed and with that, I was able to do like Charlotte did in the moment she shared in Chapter 1: I found a way to both see and see through my fear. I was able to remind myself that I do have many years of theatrical performance under my belt, and that linguistics probably did have something to bring to forensics, even though I had never thought about connecting the two before, largely since I did not know about linguistics when I was doing forensics myself back in high school.

And I am so grateful that I did! Reflecting back, that hour working with her was probably one of the most energized moments of my professional life. I can't think of another time that I drew on so many of the pieces of myself and experiences and competencies all in one moment.

When I asked her what she was wanting to do with her performance, she spoke about the challenge of finding a way to help listeners distinguish quickly and easily among the different interwoven voices in the piece, and what she was ultimately wanting to capture were subtle differences in age, region, socioeconomic status, ethnicity, and how these might shape that character's identity and world view—in short, just about everything that my close to a decade in training in variationist sociolinguistics up until that point had prepared me for.

Drawing from my more recent training in discourse analysis, I quickly conducted a sequential and distributional scan of the piece to see the order and frequency of words, phrases, and discourse units. I used this quick scan to motivate the selection of a word (or two) for each character. We then dug in with the morphology, phonology, and semantics of each selected word, interweaving her expertise as a speaker of African-American English and my academic study of the variety. I knew how to coach her as a performer, because of my experience in teaching improvisational theater and also because one of my research foci was linguistic style and dialect performance. I had been an English major in my undergrad days, and turns out, I did remember a thing or two about poetry, but most importantly, I had a few years of teaching under my belt just enough to have begun to learn that my job was to give her some tools and then get out of the way—just hold some space for her to find her voice and her way in and through the piece.

I ended by making a plug for her to consider taking a linguistics class!

This practice of reminding myself of my training to stay present is something that I summon nowadays as a language and communication consultant. Invariably, clients show up with overwhelming and unrealistic expectations about what I can actually do for them, and which I can also often see are not what they actually need. Seven years in, and I still have to summon this daily!

And so, in this chapter, I want to play with the idea of being now and here, fully embracing how sometimes that can honestly feel like being in the middle of nowhere!!

As you'll read, the stories in this chapter feature linguists finding employment of their skills in the here and now, in situations both expected and unexpected, happening at work and outside. I hope that listening to these stories in addition to sparking ideas—as with all of the stories in this book—might also remind us of the ways in which we ourselves can be more present to the affordances of the here and now. Remembering our training can give us new ways of thinking about workplace challenges, and might make us more available and present in the moment to recognize that feelings of being an imposter might be at least partly about being stretched to meet a challenge. And I'll share more ideas in the activity at the end of the chapter as well.

We'll start by playing with the idea of now, and see how "now" can be thought about in not only the short term, but also very LONG! Laura Welcher's work at the Long Now Foundation fosters longer-term thinking (at the scale of 10,000 years). There are certain kinds of questions that thinking in that timeframe engenders, for example, our responsibility for things like the world's languages which are currently going extinct. Then, we move to Kathryn Campbell-Kibler who embodies her commitment to equality and social justice when the moment calls her to allyship through small acts of bystander activism—diffusing an instance of hate speech on the bus. We'll then move to linguistics being employed at the doctor's office by Laurel Sutton. Serena Williams will share how an awareness of language policy and planning literature helps her do genealogical research, and how genealogical work—instead of being about the there and then—is actually about the here and now in many ways. And we'll finish with stories from Mackenzie Price and Marie-Ève Monnin reflecting on the current social and political moment and what it can tell us about the things we aren't doing (but could be) in our workplaces.

In some sense, this chapter (and the thinking it is intended to engender) is all about where preparation meets opportunity: Being present to the affordances of the moment means being here and now (even if it feels disorienting), so that you can then ask: What comes next? What aspect of my linguistics training might I employ here?

Laura Welcher

The Long Now

Laura Welcher is the Director of Operations for the Long Now Foundation, an organization that seeks to "creatively foster social responsibility" in the framework of the next 10,000 years. Projects at the Long Now focus on "whatever may be helpful for thinking, understanding, and acting responsibly over long periods of time." The philosophy of the organization is embodied in a precisely engineered and self-correcting clock, the brainchild of founding board member Stewart Brand, which gives the year in five digits, so 2020 is 02020. It has been specially designed to serve as a mechanism and a metaphor for reframing thinking.

When I arrived for our meeting, I realized that I had been to the organization's headquarters before, only I didn't realize that it was the headquarters of a cultural institution. I thought it was a bar. That's because it is. It is also a bar. Called The Interval. It's both. The ground floor of the organization is a bar, which they use to host events and it's where they house their library and many of the artifacts and various prototypes of the 10,000-year clock. When Laura arrived for our conversation, I told her that hands-down, having a full-service bar within a foundation's headquarters is one of the most creative ways of engaging in outreach. Handcrafted cocktails are a great tactic for getting people to slow down, warm up, and stay for a while, and that is exactly what I did!

Laura came to the Long Now about fifteen years ago to work for the Rosetta Project, which involves building a massive database called the Rosetta Disk, linking the vocabulary of all the world's languages. It's a digital database, featuring 1,500 languages and 13,000 microscopic pages of language documentation. A smaller version of it (with 1,000 pages of language information) exists in wearable analog form—Laura wears it as a necklace—it is a conversation starter. It gets people thinking about language. Why language? Well, because language is one of the longest-lived human systems. It allows cultures to persist over huge transitions, because it is a consistently evolving and changing system. It is also a means of encoding lived experience. In the course of making this digital library of all human languages publicly accessible, Laura found herself doing some deep thinking about designing and structuring the database and realized that there is a drastic difference between preserving information and preserving meaning.

In a talk about her work that she gave at "The Interval" as part of an organizational charette (which we can now feel very good about looking to Wikipedia to define: "any collaborative session in which a group of designers drafts a solution to a design problem"). Laura shares some of the questions that thinking about language preservation on this timescale has engendered for her, as I will now discuss. The link to her talk is in the references. I highly recommend viewing it so you can get a sense for the bar and event space. If you look carefully, you might also glimpse the database necklace that Laura is wearing.

Her talk presents a thought experiment: imagine that we wanted to preserve the Jack and the Beanstalk story such that someone could find it and appreciate it and crucially, know what it means centuries into the future. First, we would need to think about storage. We might choose one of the "store-everything forever" media technologies that are currently under development (Laura mentioned that the developers of these technologies often come to the Long Now

Foundation for counsel), or we could decide to use nano-manipulating quartz structures or encode the information in DNA. Either way, we are left with the problem that the person who finds it centuries from now would need to know that there is information stored there, and they would need to know how to access it. Finally, they would also need to know that the encoding is multiply embedded: that this is a digital representation in a binary system of a writing system which has been used to encode spoken language, a system—language itself—which also encodes human experience.

And even if we did manage to encode something that lasted hundreds or even thousands of years, and the finder was able to access and decode through all the layers, how would they understand what a giant is? Would they be able to appreciate what the character of Jack represents as a trickster? Doubtless, much of the cultural significance and meaning would have become disembodied and disencultured over the passage of time. What, then, does this tell us about language and how is it embodied and encultured?

Which points to the here and now of the work, which is that of ensuring a broader understanding of language and how it means and what it does and why it matters. As Laura said, "for language to have meaning, it must be lived." It represents lived experience and stores knowledge, but it is precarious and ephemeral and easily lost. Thus, the work that she does ultimately isn't about saving languages, it's about making a better context for them now. Her work is to help create a better environment for linguistic diversity to be seen as a benefit to humanity instead of as a threat. In a healthy society, meaning is created by all of the things that humans do including the knowledge of lived experience that gets contained and stored in our language. For Laura, our vibrant linguistic and cultural diversity is in fact a manual for civilization, and as such, language should always be in critical dialogue with experience—each providing critical support for the other.

Embodiment ended up being one of the broader themes of the conversation I had with Kathryn Campbell-Kibler, a professor of linguistics who spoke with me for this book at a moment of tremendous professional successes co-occurring with family and health challenges. She recently got her first NSF grant after ten years while at the very same time experiencing the longest flare-up of chronic fatigue syndrome—year and a half. "If I only have so much time and energy" she concludes: "I want to put it into what matters most—and for me, that's addressing social justice issues." So what does that look like in practice? How does Kathryn work like a linguist in addressing inequity?

We'll begin with a moment of bystander activism on a bus.

Kathryn Campbell-Kibler

Speaking Up, Being Heard

"Sir, I'm gonna need you to calm down."

These were the words Kathryn Campbell-Kibler repeated when the guy on the bus got in her face and said, "What did you say to me?" On the bus, she had overheard him using hate speech, and while it was scary and uncomfortable, as someone who has been involved in bystander intervention trainings for years now, she knew that speaking up was what she needed to do. Kathryn has been involved in the Columbus, Ohio Chapter of Standing Up for Racial Justice (SURJ) as a trainer for years now, and—as she wryly acknowledged: "If you're going to go around telling people that they should be doing this, you should do it yourself." So, when she suddenly found herself confronted with a situation that called for action, after thinking about it for a moment, asking herself, "What are the words?" she channeled her mother, an education researcher and lifelong social activist who worked doing voter registration in the 1960s and who raised her with a strong social justice drive and sense of responsibility to community.

Evincing calm, Kathryn spoke up.

The man had been muttering about someone who he thought was being disruptive. He was addressing his comments—which were becoming increasingly racialized—to a younger African-American man who was singing and making noise. "I'm doing this for all of us," his actions seemed to be conveying—that he was maintaining the social order by communicating to this person that he did not belong, did not deserve to take up space.

She decided that she needed to convey, "No, I think you're the one out of line."

After getting in her face, he did finally quiet down. He eventually sat down and stopped harassing the other passenger.

Reflecting back, she had two thoughts about the experience: (1) "OK, I'm pretty sure that I did what I wanted to do," and (2) "Wish it felt better." But sometimes the experience of embodying our values doesn't actually feel good in the moment. It doesn't feel good to be publicly out of role, and of course everyone else on that bus was avoiding eye contact and trying to pretend like nothing was happening. It would have been so much easier not to say anything, to adhere to the "don't engage the visibly agitated person" social norm, but at that moment, Kathryn decided that embodying her values meant fighting the socialization that she—as have many of us, especially women—had internalized to want to please people and not make people upset.

But as someone who has been training white allies to act as part of a multiracial majority for racial justice, Kathryn has been thinking about public space behavior for many years now. Because of this work, Kathryn finds that she is starting to inhabit the world differently, having decided that social anxiety is no longer demographically appropriate. But that doesn't mean that it's easy, either.

At an annual meeting of the Linguistics Society of America—the professional association for linguists in the United States—as part of a panel that she had spoken on the day before about creating more inclusive culture for our field, including—perhaps especially—at our professional meetings, Kathryn hosted a practice space for us (her colleagues) to try to put language to some of the suggested practices for speaking up in the moment when we experience bias. To make it hands-on, Kathryn gave us a handout, full of sample language to use in moments where an opportunity to reflect presented itself, practicing "calling in" instead of "calling out." Many of these conversation starters used who we are and how we do things, for example "we're working at hearing input from multiple perspectives" or "we want to make sure that everyone's experience gets heard."

Kathryn is a professor of linguistics, and she got the words "your first job is to free someone else" tattooed when she got tenure. These words from Toni Morrison remind her that as a professor, she has power. She recognizes that being a professor is a prestige role and she looks for ways in which she can "break off pieces of prestige" to share. Thus, it is that while she works *as* a linguist, I also see the way she uses insight about the power of language to shape experience as working *like* a linguist. I'll explore some of the various ways in which Kathryn does this as a professor, reflecting the multifaceted nature of the job in work with students, her colleagues, and the public.

She used the analogy of "triage," which she first heard from activist Kate Borenstein. If we take the term from how it is used in a medical context, it means asking not only who is in need of the most immediate help, it's also about "where can I make the best difference?" If I act now, and given who I am. As a woman, Kathryn has found that female students tend to click with her, and when she looks at our field, she sees women of color as being drastically underrepresented in positions of power and influence. Kathryn has a chronic illness, but, focusing on the question "What are female students of color missing out on?" helps her focus her energy on supporting students who have been underrepresented in positions of power. She directly sees ways of being and doing things that are worthwhile, and it's something concrete she can hold on to when ill.

For example, Kathryn has set up a summer program with the recent NSF grant, which gives undergraduates direct first-hand experience as researchers. She offers stipend slots for students of color, first-generation college students, and students looking to transfer to Ohio State University. Young folks who participate in the program benefit from the experience, but they also benefit from the network. They get introduced to people who can serve as mentors, and who have access to future opportunities. There are lunches with deans and donors and other bigwigs in the university community. Affording young people the chance to practice having conversations with people in positions of power, to really feel what those conversations feel like, sets them up for better experiences in future interactions such as job interviews, salary, and other professional negotiations. They also leave with a line on their CV or resume that says "NSF intern"—experience that looks very appealing to gatekeepers who make admissions and acceptance decisions at colleges and universities.

Finally, Kathryn is committed to producing resources for scientific researchers to understand the science behind communication. This is especially important in the case of communicating about ideas that change systems that don't want to be changed. Talking about bias often means encountering bias in order to be able to talk about it in the first place. She shares a great handout called: "Why don't they hear what I say?"as an introduction to the concept of gender ideology on her website www.FairerScience.org

Kathryn's story demonstrates that we can bring what we know about how language works to embody our values in moments when those are threatened. It serves as a reminder to speak up, and also the reminder to not expect that it is going to be easy, nor is it likely to feel good in the moment (or even immediately afterwards). But as Kathryn's story—and Laurel's story next—will demonstrate, one resource we can draw on in these moments is the deep knowledge we have about language, how it does things in interactions, and why that matters.

Laurel Sutton

Advocating for Health

From my conversation with Laurel, the image that stuck with me was her advocating for herself and for her family at the doctor's office, which brought me back to the scholarly research that I know her for: language and gender. I first got to know Laurel Sutton's name and work by reading *Reinventing Identities*, an edited volume that she worked on when she herself was a grad student. In our conversation, I heard a strong theme of awareness of the role of gender in everyday interactions, from which I draw a link to her decades of linguistic research on the subject.

In doctor–patient interactions, there is built-in knowledge and power differential, and tremendous bureaucracy that pulls toward standardization, and pressure that cuts away at listening, not to mention gender dynamics at play that as a linguist Laurel has researched for decades and in many settings. She shared an experience that she had while pregnant, when she was sick all the time, and she learned later that what she had is a genetic disorder called Ehlers-Danlos syndrome, which affects the connective tissue. However, before they had this diagnosis, she just kept hearing "well, pregnant women have morning sickness." She remembers feeling gaslit and thinking, "Can you actually die of heartburn?" She was told to do yoga and eat crackers, and was given Nexium and formulaic advice, but she was not being taken seriously by her medical team.

Always the advocate, as she shared this experience with me, she shared some magic words for the reader—words that patients can use to break through when they feel as though they are not being heard by medical professionals: "This is affecting my quality of life." In the medical context, such language gets heard differently than do descriptive statements like "This makes me really tired." As the President of the American Name Society, she convenes research conversations about language in medical encounters, such as a recent panel looking at names of medical procedures for intersex people, as part of larger conversations about names, naming, gender, sex, and the LGBTQI experience. As Laurel said "We need more linguistic research into areas like this."

And, Laurel knows a bit about the role that names play in creating identity and meaning. In 1998, or "once upon a time" as she says to begin her LinkedIn summary, she co-founded a naming firm called Catchword. Catchword brings linguistic expertise to designing names and is known for Asana (the workplace productivity platform), Upwork (the platform for freelance work), and the Chobani Flip (the yogurt line that comes with a side-compartment you flip open to add mix-ins like toasted almonds). Catchword sometimes also develops taglines for organizations like the Asian-American Civic Association, "Educate. Empower. Employ," to describe the variety of services and advocacy activities they undertake. Laurel finds that she derives a real sense of satisfaction from using the set of skills that she spent a decade cultivating while training as a linguist. There is an immediacy and sense of recognition and pride when you can see your work up on a billboard, when you know that you came up with something good for the client, something that does what it is supposed to do.

Laurel stepped down as a Catchword partner a few years ago and is now bringing linguistic analysis to a range of clients, including in the capacities of expert witness in legal contexts, marketing strategist, and personal and professional mentoring for professionals. As the convener of the Special Interest Group Linguistics Beyond Academia for the Linguistics Society of America (LBA SIG), Laurel is also advocating for health. Healthy relationships to work. She is committed to helping linguists find meaningful work in healthy, supportive environments, because from her perspective, too often, work is tied to abusive and toxic environments. This commitment spurs her on to regularly organize opportunities for linguists to talk about their work in communities of career linguists committed to exploring what is possible, what is acceptable, and how to insist on finding satisfaction and purpose in work. Laurel has always valued work—she came from a family where working was important, and where you were expected to get a job as soon as you could—but now, after working for many years and owning her own business, she feels called to make a difference for her community. Reflecting back on the changing meaning of work over the course of her own life she observed, "Everyone should have to work at McDonalds [because] it instills what it is that many people have to do to earn a living in American society. It's unfair that human worth is so tied to wealth, and it's compounded by how much we as a society undervalue the kind of work that so many people do just to stay alive." But, working during high school, college, and grad school (Laurel's stint in the service industry also comprised a year at an ice cream shop, at a music store, and as a bartender) taught her how to juggle multiple competing priorities, how to keep things flowing, how to follow procedure. Critically she also learned that there were approved ways to break the rules. There were ways to go above and beyond too, but there were some rules you just had to follow. This instilled a sense of boundaries, and work values, and at the same time a deep understanding that American society is set up such that one has to work for things.

Speaking of cultural systems, contexts, and ways of organizing experience, as we will hear in our next story from Serena Williams, genealogy starts with having a curiosity now about something in the past, your place in the world, your identity. Serena notes a significant change in how people have used genealogical research over time. While it often used to be about establishing some claim to a lineage, nowadays, its more so that people can create a sense of coherence, an interest in social history. And she hastens to add that there are plenty of reasons to do genealogy work that have nothing to do with the past. For example, taking up a curiosity about genealogy might just mean choosing to put some work now into documenting more of your life for posterity. Genealogy can be about doing the personal work to decide that your stories are worth sharing, choosing to see connection—deciding to look for ways that your life is shaped by broader forces of time and place, future and the past as you understand them.

Serena Williams

Walking in the Footsteps of Your Ancestors

Serena is a consummate researcher, and she brings that to the work that she does for the company she founded called Chronos Heritage Services, a genealogy and genealogy travel services company where she takes people on journeys to walk in the footsteps of their ancestors. The connections to her training in linguistics are everywhere, but perhaps most evident in the language policy lens that she brings to the work.

"It's a way into solving problems," she told me, as in one puzzle that presented in a recent client project. This was an ancestor profile, a narrative report profiling an ancestor in sociohistorical context. Her clients typically choose an immigrant ancestor, what American genealogists call the "gateway ancestor"—the person who came over to the United States, where Serena is based. The immigrant ancestor that was the focus of this particular project had come to the United States at the turn of the twentieth century, and while Serena was able to collect a large number of documents, she noticed that he had listed both his country of birth and his language inconsistently. In one document it appears he was born in Germany and in another it says Hungary. The puzzling thing was that she knew that these would have been self-reported because of the document types (immigration forms, ships manifests, censuses). But her prior work in social positioning theory helped her think through document contexts to know the myriad factors that might shape how someone might answer census questions, for example. Serena knew, from her research into practices of the time that census-takers around the turn of the century used to walk from house to house and would typically interview the head of household without requiring any supporting evidence for place of birth, age, or occupation, etc. The relationship of the ancestor to the head of household provides one means of evaluating the information given. Another factor to keep in mind would be that the head of household might be considering what his interlocutor knows and doesn't know about European geopolitics. Especially during WWI and WWII, a head of household might assume that the census-taker would have a strong opinion about certain regions of the world, which might shape the answers.

Serena ended up with documentation on the US side featuring the above-mentioned high degree of variability in use of referring terms but nothing from Europe. But she was tipped off when she saw a document that listed "Yugo/Slavia" as this ancestor's country of origin, because representing the country in that way points to a very particular moment in history when people were still figuring out what the name for this country would be. While all these clues pointed to the Austro Hungarian Empire, narrowing down the region of origin to the former Yugoslavia led her to search modern-day Serbian archives and to eventually locate the European records that were missing.

She employed linguistic knowledge in putting these self-reported linguistic origin statements alongside what you can see in terms of what's happening in history. In the passenger records in the immigration forms his reported language is Hungarian, and yet his surname is German-sounding. She found some newspaper classifieds in which he'd placed an ad to look for an assistant in his bakery, and he refers to himself as a "German baker." So she begins to ask herself, "Well, is he German by former nationality? Is he German by language? By ethnicity?" Having studied language contact and language policy and planning, she knows very well that people are often bilingual if they live in border towns. And she remembered Susan Gal's article, "Hungarian Peasants Can't Get Wives" where women in these border towns preferred German in terms of their multilingualism so that they could find German-speaking husbands from across the Austrian border. These Austrian men tended to be from more urban areas and that life was easier than working on a farm. Using this knowledge about language preferences and language loss as it shaped bilingualism in this area, informed by socioeconomic factors, Serena comes up with a hunch to start solving the puzzle: maybe he lived on the border between Austria and Hungary.

From this "What if?" she's able to move on to "Ok, let's suppose that during his early years in Europe, he spoke German at home, and then he knew Hungarian for talking in the community, let's just say that that's the way it was because he was on the border." She looked up the language policy and planning of the Austro-Hungarian empire. As a unified empire, it allowed both languages, but the implication was that towns would often have two names—one in Hungarian, and one in German. This was it! The was the key she needed! Searching for the town name in Hungarian led her to find his baptism record in archives in Budapest. She followed a hunch to find that Hungarian record about a Catholic church in a town that is today located in Austria, and which has a completely different name in Hungarian than it does in German. In German, the town is called Großpetersdorf but in Hungarian it is called Szent Mihály.

Having identified his place of birth, she was then able to track how he moved around the Empire over the course of his life, and to form another hunch—that he might have been in the military. After being born in modern-day Eastern Austria (as she learned in the baptism record), she found a marriage record that showed he lived in modern-day Serbia in his twenties, and then learned that he lived in modern-day Hungary just before emigrating to the United States by a baptismal record of a child.

A map for those of you who are so inclined, to think about these geopolitical entities as they are understood in the here and now (Figure 4.2).

We can see how linguistics proved to be an extremely helpful lens for understanding this genealogical puzzle!

And now for another puzzle, this one in the domain of organizational culture.

Mackenzie Price

The Questions We Don't Ask in the Workplace

When I caught up with Mackenzie Price, she was just beginning a book about how we talk (and what we're not saying) at work. This was late June 2020, and she was feeling like the present moment

FIGURE 4.2 *Serena Williams Map © OpenStreetMap Contributors (available under the Open Database License)*

was calling her to reengage with her dissertation, where she looked at the linguistic strategies used to enact power in professional interactions among colleagues. She shared that this national moment of reckoning about race and racial equity was calling to her as a person of color to create a resource—something small and easy-to-use for professionals—something smart about talking. Something that you could grab at the airport and read on a short plane ride.

In her words:

The idea has been on my mind for a while,
but as I look at this particular moment
and the last few weeks in June that have seen a lot of an uptick
and maybe who knows if it will plateau or uptick or down again
thinking about inclusion and diversity
and the fact that inequity exists,
And even underneath all of that,
Hints that the society is going to talk about the fact
that Black people see different things, think different things,
experience different things that—for lack of a better word—
dominant society does not know about.

Juneteenth being a great example. There's a population that has a different independence day. Much of the conversation around the event in the weeks surrounding it in 2020 had been about who already knew about the day and who didn't, but Mackenzie's invitation was to stop and reflect on this for a moment: In a country that's all about freedom, some people celebrate a different independence day.

She continued:

I got into my dissertation because I was interested in language and work
And workplaces
Something I've been thinking about is that idea
That there are people
From my vantage point—Black people—who are thinking, seeing, talking about and not talking about different things than what everybody else is talking about.
Is something that workplaces can wake up to.

As our conversation unfolded, we talked about how being "a linguist, and a sociolinguist, and an interactional sociolinguist" makes Mackenzie aware that people have different ways of using language. Factors like language policy and practice and politics, the history of social stratification by race, the fact that multiple metamessages can be sent by the same cue, and the ways that people misunderstand each other, are crystalizing for Mackenzie into the question: "What are the things that employers are not asking their employees?" A question about a question.

At the time of our conversation, there was also a proliferation of "how to" advice that came in the wake of the shift to remote work because of the Covid pandemic encouraging people to "ask more questions at work." However, as we discussed, this advice can be hard to put into practice and can actually be quite dangerous. Some kinds of questions build solidarity, others won't. It depends. On lots of things. In the academic literature, questions are often analyzed as control devices, and as opportunities to assert power in institutional and professional settings (e.g., Ehrlich and Freed, 2010). For example, a question can influence the topic of subsequent turns with the introduction of new themes that are relevant to the speaker's expertise or interest.

Asking questions about questions needs a linguist. It demands knowledge about context and nuance, and I'm so glad that Mackenzie is doing so!

Her dissertation analysis comprised myriad features including positioning, reference, dialogic voicing, narratives, intertextuality, and frames, exploring how this constellation of linguistic features get utilized to enact power and control in the Executive Education classroom. She investigated discursive genres like class discussions and persuasive presentations as contexts where students can act powerfully and create asymmetries among peers. But it is her last analysis chapter—the one that focuses on question and answer sessions—that I want to focus on here. Because she chose to focus on the questions that don't happen, but could.

And why.

Mackenzie's data were collected from student presentations, and she zeroed in on the moment when the presenter had finished their presentation and the floor opened for Q&A. In the moment, as she was taking field notes, she observed that often, their classmates did not ask them questions. Instead, many took the opportunity to provide commentary. When she sat down to analyze her data, what she found was these would-be questioners did employ interrogative syntax, but that what they said could best be interpreted as advice-giving rather than questioning. While the floor is ceded in such contexts for the purposes of asking questions, speakers chose to enact leadership and power as they "use these opportunities to lay claim to knowledge about successful business practices." Such a display of expertise "not only enacts power but also creates asymmetries of knowledge and experience between students" (112).

In the dissertation, Mackenzie drew the parallel to her academic life, noting that "academics are called upon to share their subject matter expertise at events like academic presentations, but frequently find that it is challenged or is used as a backdrop for a colleague sharing his or her own expertise in order to index membership in a wider community of experts." A display in front of a gathered community of experts. At the time of our conversation in June 2020, Mackenzie had been working as a professional trainer and facilitator for a number of years, and she drew the parallel to the questioning she has experienced in her professional capacity in front of other rooms full of experts. As someone who is quite attuned to the dance of epistemic rights, which take place when space is given to questions, she knows which questions to acknowledge—and how—including acknowledging a question but not answering it. This can be especially true for women and people of color. Given that her job is to convey knowledge, there are times where questions literally interfere with being able to do her job.

Mackenzie's idea to bring academic insights together with her professional experience to the broader business world is valuable and much-needed as a research and data-informed approach. It's one thing to observe that questions can be used—and are—as clarification tools, which can be (but aren't always) interpreted as being helpful and cooperative. They can also be used to do things like "upgrade or downgrade epistemic authority"—a person's "rights, responsibilities and obligations to know" (Heritage and Raymond, 2005, 2006). The absence of questions can also be heard as a very noisy not.

Here and now in 2020, Mackenzie's intersectional attention to the questions that leaders could be asking their employees, and that colleagues could be asking one another:

> I think it would be a revolutionary thing if in the context of work relationships
> if people asked "what is it like to be not-white in this workspace?"
> or "what does it feel like to be not a man in this workspace?"

As she notes, no one is asking questions like these, but doing so would help move what people experience in workspaces in terms of policy and practice. Because it is through language that institutions work: Through the actions people take, the things that people say, all of the structures that make up a workplace context. If people are given the opportunity to talk about and crucially given the opportunity to be heard—how might this transform the ways that they experience all of these aspects of institutional life?

Simply allowing room for this curiosity means something. And following that by asking the question could start conversations about what contributes to the experience that many African Americans report of feeling visible and not visible at the same time. It might prompt more questions like "What documents and interactions and pieces of communication contribute to that lived experience in this workplace?"

To close out our conversation, Mackenzie shared a couple ways that having thought about questions helps her and which might be empowering to others: The first is that questions don't always get answers, they get responses. If you are being asked a question that you don't want to answer for whatever reason, you have choices. And the other is that asking questions about questions can help us navigate the workplace, that asking ourselves when questions get asked, who asks them, in what contexts, helps us gain insight into what questions are DOING in the workplace. Equipped with this knowledge, employees can more easily recognize what kind of relationships these are functioning in service of to help them decide how they want to participate, and—back to her first idea—how to respond.

Marie-Ève, whose attention was called to the urgent need for language access and advocacy for immigrants to the United States (as she is herself), found that this called her to quit her job as a Spanish assistant professor.

Marie-Ève Monnin

Structural Humility

When I caught up with Marie-Ève, she was just learning about a new term: "Structural Humility" in preparation for a guest lecture she was giving at McGill University for her former professor. She wanted to link Indigenous Studies—what she used to focus on academically—with film studies and language access, the work she does now. She connected to the concept structural humility because it complements cultural competence. Having previously done work in cross-cultural competency, and intercultural dialogue she found that these approaches were very focused on individual interactions, but don't change the structure or the system. She came to feel that the approach was insufficient because it tends to forget about the economics. Economic empowerment is linked to cultural empowerment. Structural competency looks to how this might be accomplished.

Her interest has always been in economic empowerment, and how it's linked to cultural empowerment. As she shared, "It's one thing to celebrate people's cultures, but if you don't empower them to be able to live those components freely, fully, because they're struggling to eat and to support their families, then it's really difficult. So those two things are very much together." She finds it more difficult in the United States—she moved here in 2014 from Canada—because everything is focused on culture and on race, and people tend to forget the intersection with economics, and with politics. "You can't just silo those things and not think about everything else."

She gave as an example some work she was reading about by engaged scholars and researchers working with a Labor agency in California, exploring how this agency communicated with farmworkers about their rights, about their agency, and about their possibilities to fight for those rights. When they looked at the systems of communication to the farmworkers, what they found is that all the materials were in Spanish. And that most of them were online. Both choices were contraindicated by the population to whom they were targeting this information, most of whom were indigenous with varying levels of literacy in Spanish, most of whom did not have easy and regular access to the internet. Reading is linked to levels of education, and access to education is linked to race, but it's also linked to economics.

She liked this example because it shows how it's not enough to just look at culture when it comes to thinking about accessing written information. Researchers also need to think about access to financial resources, taking into consideration everything that comes along with being able to send kids to school or to be able to go to school themselves (if they're working fourteen or fifteen hours a day in the fields, they don't have time to go to school to learn English or Spanish). Further, for the research participant who did have levels of literacy that allowed them to understand Spanish, they probably had maybe thirty dollars a month to spend on their mobile phones to pay for data. Accessing websites, tutorials, and videos cost so much money, that if they just did that once over the month, their thirty dollars were gone, and they didn't have access to their phone for the rest of the month. And so the choice between having access to their phone for the month for emergencies, being able to or communicate with community and with family, or using it to learn about their rights, isn't really much of a choice ultimately. Structural competence is understanding how the system works, and how it's not working.

She connected with this concept because she saw how well it reflected the work she does to bridge communities as part of the language access and advocacy organization she created called Creating Puentes.

Marie-Ève formed Creating Puentes in May 2019 in response to the increasingly alarming immigration crisis throughout the United States. She saw language access as a way to help. Her focus thus far has been with legal nonprofits, offering translation services to bridge some of the gaps that she saw—for example, much of the legal staff were bilingual, but if they were spending all of their time translating necessary documents—such as credible fear interviews, for example—that's less time providing legal services.

Structural humility gives her a new way of understanding and developing her approach to the work. When it comes to language access, she wants to bring structural humility to her thinking about the impacts to the communities that she is working to support. Talking with those communities, she wants to find out how language access doesn't work, because of questions of access, because of questions of financial, economic hardship, levels of education, added to race and ethnicity and things like cultural characteristics. She sees the approach as being very complimentary with cultural competency, because once you have the first level, then people can start looking at the structure they're in. It's a way of seeing.

As part of a recent project, Marie-Ève worked with conference organizers to think through their event design considering language access—or a language approach—as another way to look at diversity, equity, and inclusion. She found that they had something like twenty per cent of non-native English speakers in attendance at the conference. Out of the eighty per cent, there was probably around sixty or seventy per cent that spoke no other language than English. And so she said, "What that tells me is that you have a problem of diversity among your attendees, because diversity isn't just a question of race. Yes, it definitely is a component. But linguistic diversity also points to different types of experiences, different types of knowledges different types of backgrounds, even if a person was born here. If they speak Spanish at home, I can guarantee you that their experiences growing up are going to have been very different from a person who speaks English at home." They had never considered it that way. For Marie-Ève, this work is not just about representation, like physical representation, it's about so much more.

Although Marie-Ève herself is not a linguist by training, I think anyone who has studied linguistics can see the connection to work in language access. I hope this sparks connections such that readers can perhaps see themselves in this work. There is a great need, and her commitment demonstrates that there is room for all of us in the work of building inclusive communities together.

Recalling the now/here campaign that I used to introduce the chapter, Marie-Ève's story, along with the other stories here, we have considered different ways that linguists (and non-linguists who work like linguists) become aware of being called to use linguistics in the present moment.

To close this chapter, I thought we could look at some strategies for staying in the now/here even when—especially when—you are feeling like you're in the middle of nowhere!

A Catalyst for You: Some Practices for Being in the Now/Here

Career can be an intensely anxious proposition. We all want to do something that brings meaning and purpose to our lives and for many of us, work will be a primary means through which we seek to make a difference in the world. Feeling like there is a great deal riding on the decisions that we make, especially at times of transition (just starting out, changing jobs, changing careers, or simply contemplating any of the above), we add pressure, when we are already feeling lost. And while I want to acknowledge the anxiety—it is all too real—at the same time, we can't let it get in the way of the task at hand. And it certainly will if we let it.

We need to let it be.
And be
where we are,
now/here.

But how do we do this?

Well, since we can't know what is coming down the pike, and we can't change what is past, the task kind of defines itself: stay present to what is here and now. You task is to figure out which of the opportunities currently in front of you are ones that you would like to pursue. AND if there are no opportunities, how you might stir some up! *Even if we do have opportunities, it's probably always a good idea to be stirring them up ...*

And, being mindful that this is something that we are going to be figuring out for our entire working lives, I figured the best way to end this chapter would be to share some practices, starting with gratitude.

Express Gratitude

Now, certainly I'm not the only one out there talking about gratitude, but there is a very real place for such a practice when it comes to career. No matter where you are, someone helped you get there. Someone in your community (who you know or don't know yet) inspired you with their work or their words, in any one of a million ways. Someone is out there advocating for you, whether you know about it or not. In *Bringing Linguistics to Work* I talk about the gracious note, basically sending some appreciative thoughts to someone— maybe someone whose article you used recently which helped you build an argument. In that book, I share the story of a gracious note that led me to meet Camilla Vasquez, with whom I have collaborated on a few projects now, and who I now consider to be my friend! In the *Thank You Project: Cultivating Happiness One Letter of Gratitude at a Time*, Nancy Davis Kho talks about writing a letter to the person who designed the assistive technology that was helping her to be able to walk as she recovered from an injury. This is what we're going for, because just like that, you have already begun the next practice: honoring community.

Honor Community

For most of us, our networks will be how we find most of our professional opportunities moving forward. And networking really is something that bears thinking about in the here and now, because networking in a way that honors community is not just about now, it is about building trust and trusting for the long haul. It is about sharing, and it is about being generous. It is about giving other people opportunities to be generous. When we invest in building and supporting our community now, we help ourselves. Start with the people who currently surround you. If you are a student, think about what you can do to support and connect with your classmates.

One of the many reasons your community is invaluable to you is that others are in a better position than you are to notice the patterns in the ways that your gifts and ways of thinking and working tend to express themselves.

Listen for Patterns

Pattern recognition in community is behind the design of many of the structures that I use to support career, including Pocket Full of Stories, the Mighty Network, and Career Camp, where we cultivate story-listening abilities so as to be able to notice patterns in expressions of curiosity: the work contexts that you find yourself drawn to comprise expressions of where and with whom you feel called to share your gifts. Cultivating your story-listening abilities will help you be more tuned-in to these patterns for yourself, but also the gift of listening is helpful to your community. Story listening then becomes a way to be generous (see how this works? Each one of these supports the others).

Go for "being curious with." And aim to: Receive, Reflect with questions like: "tell me more about" or "why do you think you chose to do X?" or "I could imagine someone else doing Y, what did that choice mean to you?"

Your perspective as story listener is invaluable because storytellers can't know what is not clear to others if it is not clear to them. Offering your perspective can illuminate things that are genuinely unclear, confusing, or in need of elaboration. Reflective listening can also be a tool for countering bias, and "calling-in" as we have been discussing throughout the book.

Be Generous

Spend an hour on LinkedIn looking for ways to pay it forward. Who in your community is asking for something? ("help me spread the word about ___", etc.) with whom might you share a resource that you just came across in your newsfeed? Who might benefit from a connection or an opportunity right now?

Research has shown that generosity has very positive effects for anxiety. This was probably at play in the forensics story that I used to begin this chapter. Focusing on what someone else needs can be tremendously beneficial for you both.

5

BRIGHTEN Around the World

In Chapter 4, we invoked the idea of the "here and now," using "now/here" as a reminder to not only pay attention to where we are, and increase our comfort with discomfort, but also to broaden the timescales of our thinking. In this chapter, we'll take off from "here" to consider "there"—by listening to stories from around the world, realizing ultimately how very interconnected we all are, and considering how these might help us think about our shared future as a planet.

As the stories reveal, the big things needed to successfully collaborate internationally (or as an international person coming to work in the United States) seem to be helpful in all contexts: Listening, paying attention to inclusion, flexibility in thinking, asking "why can't we?" and refusing to let "can't be done" stand, making room for complexity, and both/and rather than either/or thinking.

We'll begin with Mika Hama, whose experience traveling back and forth between the United States and Japan for the past few years has brought her to new levels of appreciation for the power of listening. We'll gain some insight into the e-commerce realm from Serena P who finds use for her study of multiple languages in her work in global search marketing. Former professor Kay Gonzales shows us how starting a business is like doing a PhD. And we'll conclude with a few stories of activism and advocacy. We'll start with Kólá Túbòsún and the Yorùbá language advocacy to which he has devoted his professional life to think about how and why we can make technology more inclusive. We'll end with a couple of stories about policy, concluding with a story from Ester Surenthiraraj whose story (captured in its unfolding) suggests some of the many additional potential applications of policy analysis.

I hope that their stories will be illuminating to both linguists who live and work in the United States, but also those who are reading this book from around the globe. The insights they share about how to be successful working internationally have everything to do with how to be more collaborative wherever you are. Such stories can be listened to as mirrors and/or windows: some reflect our own experiences back at us, others broaden our horizons by giving us a view into something new.

The activity that concludes this chapter will focus on catalyzing momentum in our own stories.

Mika Hama

Doing Listening

Mika Hama is the Director of Strategy and Innovation at Second Language Testing Inc. (SLTI), an organization with whom she has been collaborating for nearly seven years. With SLTI, and with partnerships that she has developed through this work, Mika has had the opportunity to travel, live, and work between the United States and Japan for the past several years and as such, I thought she would be a good person to start off this chapter, to help us move away from the United States—where most of our stories have been centered so far—to take a broader, more international scope. When Mika was first hired by SLTI, her first project took her to Japan, where she herself was born and raised. While in Japan, the bulk of her work was with teams in the Philippines, and now, back in the United States—much of her work is with teams located in India and Japan.

Mika's story is first and foremost an exemplification of the power of listening, and in fact, one of the first examples she shared was a demonstration of her listening abilities. Early on in her tenure with SLTI, she had been sent to Japan to work on an English test and she found herself in a room with eight English teachers "grilling" her as she put it—about the ways that changes to the test were going to change how they taught. They were pointing out that neither she nor her organization really knew what teaching was like in Japan, and therefore had brought idealistic assumptions into the test design which didn't align with the reality of the classroom. Mika listened. She found herself revisiting her PhD coursework and going back and rereading theory bearing the concerns of these practitioners in mind. By thinking through how she might reinterpret research findings in ways that would be actionable and meaningful and helpful to them, she found that she understood everything better herself. She described the feeling as a moment where it all just clicked!

This "middle way" starts with an ability to keep the broader purpose in mind while navigating the work and all the people involved in it. In Mika's words:

> Yeah, I think that the big picture was that we wanted to the test to help teachers change the way they teach.
> So if we catered too much toward what they want, what they already know, you know,
> They don't want to go too much out of their comfort zone
> We can push them
> So there are certain things we have to push them on
> "No, we have to do it this way
> This might make you uncomfortable, but the outcome is going to be this way and that is what you really want to see."

For Mika, building this middle way involved consulting practitioners, not only to seek guidance in informing the test design, but also to really listen to what the changes to the test would mean for those who use it. Crucially, Mika also wanted to put all of this into conversation with the literature to bring in her own expertise about how their teaching could change and should change so that English education would be more impactful for students. She described the things on which there cannot be compromise as "the backbone." In balancing the perspectives of teachers and test designers, her guiding motivation are recommendations that can be supported by research—by data—not just an educated guess or intuition. "If there's theories out there, we use that as a backbone."

So while it was a bit of a twist for Mika to bring her training in Applied Linguistics to this work (her training was in acquisition not assessment), there are many assumptions in assessment about how language is acquired that inform the work from a different angle. Someone with a background and training in acquisition approaches the work with a commitment and sense of professional responsibility for how test design can have very real implications on teaching and learning. This is a responsibility she takes very seriously, and makes her effective at what she does.

And her powerful listening abilities are apparent in a recent move to newer responsibilities in "developing corporate relationships and managing projects related to Artificial Intelligence and cutting-edge language learning and teaching materials," as described on her LinkedIn profile. It all started back when she was in Tokyo, working as a Second Language Acquisition specialist in an advisory capacity, doing the work described above of collaborating with an education company to put together online tests and also developing online test prep materials. Mika kept hearing that AI was going to be a bigger and a bigger part of the learning and testing experience. But from what she was hearing, it didn't seem like AI was the right way to go. However, she didn't have anything to be able to back up this opinion. She just didn't know enough about what AI was actually doing. So she thought to herself: "Okay, since we are heading in this direction, probably it makes sense to know more. I know there's probably a good way of using it, and there is a bad way of using it, but no one is out there saying, 'Ok, we need to be thinking about this, and avoiding that so that we can all get the most benefit from this technology.'" She also observed that most of the people who are currently using AI are computational-heavy, not content (language) specialists. So she decided to listen and learn.

When she got the offer to come back to the United States and SLTI were offering her the position of director, she asked, "Hey, can I do AI stuff?" Their response: "Who is going to do the AI stuff?" and Mika says, "Me. I don't know anything about AI, but I can learn!" So she started learning. She and a colleague went to the AAAI Conference on AI and talked to a bunch of people there, finally meeting a group from an AI research lab from a university in

India, and they clicked. And they started collaborating on a speaking scoring system.

And now as she learns, Mika is more and more able to advise others about how to use AI. For example, some people are very bullish on using AI because they think it introduces less subjectivity into the assessment process. "But," Mika hastens to add:

> AI is not good with meaning!
> It can see the associational words in terms of where words are collocated
> and how often those words appear,
> just to see if there is a text coherence by looking at how one word was used or how synonyms were used,
> but AI cannot understand the intention of the human,
> it doesn't know anything about the argument.

Mika notes that even though AI technology keeps improving rapidly, "we do need humans for sure with the current AI capability, and possibly for the near future."

She described a biweekly meeting with her team of ten or so data scientists working in India on testing data (the test-taker's audio as well as the human rating or score). They hold up the results from their AI-scoring models to human ratings, and in these meetings, discuss strategies for improving their scores relative to human raters, for example, knowledge of sentence segmentation techniques for spoken data. As Mika explains, a part of the creation of an AI-supported scoring system will depend on the system being trained to be able to accurately detect grammatical complexity, which in turn depends on having knowledge about sentence boundaries, structure, and flow. Mika brings familiarity with the literature about how other scholars have approached the tasks of measuring speaking abilities and developing such assessments, which help her work with her team to improve the accuracy of the AI as compared to humans. Her previous professional experience also informs the work as she can draw from knowledge about how human raters are trained, as well as what the other major testing companies do and how they do it.

Finally, Mika strongly advocates that readers must remember to make a bit of time for talking about non-work-related things with colleagues. Building relationships with the people with whom you work is especially important for working with people from different cultural backgrounds when it can be more difficult to build trust. She gave the example of her current collaborative project with folks in India. When Mika began this project, she knew that she had gaps in her knowledge about Indian popular culture, so she asked her team for recommendations for Bollywood movies to watch. Folks chimed in about their suggestions for which were classics, which were not to be missed, and the order in which she should watch them. This enabled her to begin meetings with a little check-in about her progress by way of small talk, which in turns signaled her curiosity and appreciation and interest about their cultural context as well as an openness to learning more. Mika found that demonstrating interest in people is the very best way to support the work.

To close our conversation, I invited Mika to think about what she might want to share with international readers about her perspective on working and living in the United States and also what she might want to share with readers from North America and the United States in particular about being globally minded in their approach to work. She spoke about the importance of creating a work culture of flexibility, and shared that one of the things she most values about her current organization is that there is no expectation that there should be a set way of "this is how a project goes." Deadlines and timelines are negotiated and require involvement from all parties, and there needs to be a shared awareness that you can't decide at the outset that you know how everything is going to unfold over the course of the work.

A wonderful variation on the theme of the value of being able to embrace uncertainty, an idea which gets echoed by our next storyteller Serena.

Serena P.

From Playing with Words to Playing with Keywords

Serena P. is passionate about foreign languages and the use of linguistics to make global search marketing more effective.

She's currently the Digital Marketing Manager for a multinational e-commerce company. She says that while she is still learning, every single day, "somehow I know I am in a good place because I can continue working with foreign languages while bringing my analytical skills to the next level."

She's been working in search engine marketing and pay-per-click advertising for large e-commerce brands since 2013, and lately, has been collaborating with various universities as a lecturer. For the purposes of this story, I chose to place focus on a moment in Serena's career transition when she moved from copywriter to Search Engine Marketing—a transition that Serena described as moving "from playing with words to playing with keywords."

Serena began working as a copywriter while still pursuing her Bachelor's degree, when she was looking for a part-time job that would allow her to start putting into practice what she had been studying. She admits that she had no idea copywriting was a thing— because she didn't realize that "content" meant sitting down and coming up with creative ideas—and it was a bit challenging at first. Serena had to stretch her writing skills in both Italian and English, playing with words in order to resonate with those who would read them. And when it came to choosing the word or phrases that best fit into a message, she reckons that extreme attention to the choice of words that the work demands was undoubtedly something that she was good at because of her training in Linguistics.

She worked in copywriting until she earned her Master's in Applied Linguistics at which time she felt that it was time to explore the more innovative and complex world known as Search Engine Marketing. Her work in communications and brand identity/awareness gave her the context to view this as the "what comes next" in a sales process. With search marketing you can obtain immediate results, but making target audiences perform certain actions like buying, for instance— called "conversions," in most cases, you are reaping the benefits of a previous brand awareness activity.

The transition was facilitated by a Web Marketing and Social Media Marketing course which fueled her growing interest for the digital world, but she mainly had to learn everything on the job. Which is why she tells those who are looking to break into the tech world "being eager to learn is a quality that you should be proud to show an employer." Accommodating new knowledge, and using it to solve problems or finding new ways to improve existing situations, demonstrates flexibility and adaptability. She recognizes that she was in the right place at the right time when the company was looking for fresh graduates to train in the area of web marketing, and that she was lucky to have a great mentor, but she also worked hard, learning as much as she could, amidst a period of outstanding growth at the agency, and crucially—she was able to embrace the not knowing, in order to learn new things.

At the agency, her work involved helping brands sell more online through their e-commerce channel. Her role was to make them be more easily found by specific queries on Google and other major search engines. In a nutshell, she would research which keywords best represent users' queries on search engines for specific products or brands, and then craft specific messages (search ads) to appear whenever those specific queries got typed by users in a specific country on a specific search engine. Whenever a user clicked on one of those ads, the search engine got paid for that click, pricing determined by a system that is very similar to an auction. In short, her job was about investing money to bring the right users to the right place (e.g., an e-commerce website) in order to make them perform an action there (e.g., a purchase)—something that Serena can do in multiple languages.

Having studied Russian, English, French, and with Italian as her native language, Serena had a lot to draw from in order to research keywords, write ads, and optimize advertising efforts. And, her knowledge of linguistics really came into play when she would work in languages similar to those she had studied, for example, Slavic languages such as Polish and Czech, where she could often quickly figure out the meaning of a query without having to look it up. Having said that, she hastens to add that working with localization experts is in most cases essential at all stages of this process.

Serena credits her academic studies with helping her develop a research methodology that she could apply to her everyday work: the ability to identify a phenomenon worth researching (for instance, low response to an ad), to set out the conditions to effectively analyze it (e.g., launching an A/B test, that is to say, writing two different versions of an ad), to measure the results after a predefined amount of time (e.g., ad A gets more clicks than ad B) and to draw conclusions (e.g., ad A performs better probably because it contains a price indicator in it). An example project: Serena set up a search campaign in Russia for a luxury men's clothing brand. She began by researching the best queries for this specific product in Russian, working with Yandex—the most popular Russian search engine—and writing the related ads for these queries, based on keywords like "luxury Italian men's shoes" that she got from putting herself in her future clients' shoes (if you'll forgive the pun) and trying to think like them. As she says, "Of course, you can never know how your keywords will perform until you launch your campaigns, but the work can be iterative. And there's plenty of analytics tools to measure performance and adjust a campaign accordingly."

Every day is different and includes analyzing the quality of website traffic to one or more online stores, optimizing search marketing campaigns on Google Ads, writing reports, talking to clients, or attending internal meetings. There are also regular training sessions and professional development. "It is never boring," Serena says, "working in the digital world is exciting, you're always learning. And things change so fast." She particularly enjoys working with a team that really helps one another, and though it can be stressful—the level of attention required is always high, and you need to work on several projects at the same time—the efforts eventually pay off.

I asked Serena what she would say to those readers who might be interested in following a similar path. She shared that she often feels amazed at what an unpredictable path she embarked upon after graduating in Applied Linguistics in Italy. In her words:

Let me give you some context: when I began studying at university twelve years ago, in the middle of the Great Recession, I remember my family being skeptical about me choosing to study Linguistics. I was very good at Math, and had excellent grades. My high school teachers would encourage me to apply for an Engineering degree. Most of my friends would go into Business studies. I had a plethora of options ... but, did I want to become an Engineer? Did I see myself working in a bank? I would find a job easily but that's not what I wanted. I chose to follow my passion. Was I scared? A bit. Most linguistics graduates would struggle to carve out a role for them. And yet, I was aware of my potential and I never stopped believing that, somewhere out there, I would find my place in this world. I had always enjoyed the idea of working with foreign languages, but I was also fascinated by the Internet. And I happened to have an analytical mind. I also loved teaching. What could my future role be?

The perfect job does not get served to you on a silver platter. You have to gradually find it, uncover it, pursue it. Build it. Be engaged in as many side projects as your energy and time allow. Let your passion guide you. I decided that this would be my lifetime non-negotiable: if I ever felt that something was not enriching me, and that I was not enjoying doing it, I would quit it. My advice to Linguistics graduates: let your professional path evolve side by side with your passions and interests. You will get there at some point! And when you get there, be ready to leave again and embark on new journeys. That's how I see my professional life.

To close up our conversation, I asked her to look to the future, to identify emerging trends, including changes that will impact this world of work down the road. From her perspective, search marketers will need to continue adapting to the always evolving search habits of users worldwide, as well as increasing use of AI and machine learning to optimize the entire search engine marketing process. While algorithms are getting more and more powerful, it will always be important to be there at the right time with the right message. Search marketers and advertisers will be needed to craft the right message based on the user's intent (meeting the users' needs throughout their entire customer journey). Search marketing will become more and more powerful thanks to better integration with data analytics, and it will be more and more crucial to address individual people rather than browsers (which are currently identified via cookies).

Marketers use the idea of a "customer journey" to make informed decisions about how and when and where to effectively reach out to prospective customers. In an increasingly cookieless world, there's only going to be more need for skilled researchers and people who can come up with innovative solutions to work with different sets of data. Serena also believes—and hopes—that this type of career will be chosen by translators and localization experts because she sees a great deal of potential in the combination of these two types of professions.

Serena closed by emphasizing that networking is fundamental for anyone working in the digital world. As this work sector includes many different specializations, you will surely need to build a professional network of experts to consult whenever needed.[1]

Kólá Túbòsún

Language Advocacy

Kólá Túbòsún has spent his life finding creative ways to preserve and share the Yorùbá Language, including advocacy campaigns like #TweetYoruba to get Twitter to translate the platform into Yorùbá in 2014.[2] Although anyone can theoretically tweet in any language, Kólá's campaign was about giving Yorùbá speakers the ability to experience the platform itself in Yorùbá. Seemingly small changes like seeing the buttons "follow" or "retweet" in one's own language make a tremendous difference in terms of advancing inclusion, and de-centering English. In the aim of decolonizing technology, making space for our multilingual reality will involve millions of little changes like this. As Kólá sees it, the adaptability of technology is why it plays such an important role in sustaining languages.

One of his favorite projects, YorubaName.com a Multimedia Dictionary, began as Kólá's undergraduate thesis at the University of Ibadan in 2005. He had collected approximately a thousand names in Yorùbá, and asked friends to pronounce and record them in audio form, building HTML so that users would get not only the Yoruba translation into English, but also the morphological breakdown in Yorùbá and a bit of a sense for the contextual meaning of the name. In 2015, he had a vision of creating a Wiki that would be a combination of a dictionary and an encyclopedia. It would enable people to also upload a story about their name, including family legends and meaning. He revisited the project, pulling together an Indiegogo fundraising campaign to be able to hire some collaborators. The site has become a place for English speakers to learn a bit about Yorùbá, and for Yorùbá speakers to learn more about their language and culture and heritage, something that many young people are losing touch with amidst globalizing forces that pull to English. A year later, he added an audio element, through a Yorùbá speech synthesizer he created at TTSYoruba.com. Now, users of the dictionary at YorubaName.com can also hear the names pronounced by an automated voice that Kólá created based on his own.

When I asked Kólá about what got him started in Linguistics, he said, "I could say it's serendipitous, but that would mean that all the building blocks set by parents, teachers, and other conditions around my upbringing played no part. That wouldn't be true." With hindsight, Kólá says that it feels like there was an unconscious plan all along. He was interested in languages as far back as he can remember, particularly in the tension between Yorùbá which he speaks as a first language—and which his family spoke at home—and English, which was spoken in school to the exclusion of any other language. There was an interest, but it wasn't overtly expressing itself. At first, he thought he would study Theatre Arts. And even when he came to study Linguistics, he had some misconceptions. Like many people, Kólá initially thought linguistics was about learning many new languages. But then, after the first year as an undergrad, he knew better. He discovered phonetics, phonology, morphology, sociolinguistics, and syntax and was hooked! As Kólá puts it, "[Linguistics] was enchanting, and I didn't want to go anywhere else."

And, he has taken his interest around the world. After being awarded a Fulbright to teach Yorùbá at Southern Illinois University, Edwardsville, for a year, he got his MA in Linguistics/TESL from the same university, and even wrote a collection of poems about the experience: *Edwardsville by Heart* was published in November 2016 by Wisdom's Bottom Press, UK. Currently, Kólá is at the British Library in London, as part of a year-long research fellowship working with its African languages print collection from the nineteenth century. He has worked with Google Nigeria as a Speech Linguistics Project Manager (2015–16), leading the language team that created the first Nigerian English voice assistant on Google's products for the Nigerian market; and later from February 2019 to December 2019 as a Project Manager for NLP (natural language processing) tasks in African languages. He's even been a freelance lexicographer with

Oxford University Press, UK, and was part of the team behind the last update that saw OED adding twenty-nine whopping new Nigerian English words into the dictionary. In his words:

> Most of what has brought me satisfaction as an adult has come from work with languages, doing things I love with it. Understanding how language works, and how it influences society, has helped me better appreciate the world.

Looking forward, Kólá is going to be bringing attention to writing and publishing Nigerian words with proper diacritics, a courtesy that is usually afforded to languages like French or Swedish. He argues that this is a holdover from colonialism which has denied Nigerian literature a dynamism expected from a country of so many languages, and he's hoping that his intervention makes some significant changes happen in the near future. He has also become committed to translating contemporary Nigerian (and world) literature into Yorùbá.

To see him in action advocating for language awareness and access, especially through technology, take a look at his TEDx Surelere talk, where among other things, he points out that Siri has been translated into Finnish (spoken by five million people), and Norwegian (spoken by about six million), but not yet into Yorùbá—spoken by thirty million (not to mention Hausa or Igbo). Kólá concludes his talk by reflecting on the value—now and for the future—of rethinking some of the internalized devalorization which has taken place as a result of educational policies, and to embrace the power of reimagining the relevance and reclaiming language at local, state, national, and international levels.

Kay Gonzales

What If We Approached Business Like Doing a PhD?

Kay [kai] Gonzales is the co-owner (along with his wife) of a small boutique resort—called Alberto Dorner—on the Canary Islands of Spain. They own and manage this resort with a focus on sustainability and community-involved hospitality. They try to bring in the community, hiring only local people, buying from local providers. And they work to help their guests have an immersion experience. For one thing, they have an archaeologist working in the resort who takes guests on tours—walking tours so there's no ecological footprint—explaining as they go, the history of the island and incorporating things as they are noticed. So if guests see a lizard, the guide explains everything about lizards—trees, volcanoes, ocean, geology whatever you can do in a couple hours of walking. As Kay explains, his wife runs the business day to day, and he's more focused on what we do next. He shared that he likes to say, "She runs the business as it is today, I prepare the next five years."

Since the 1980s, the Canary Islands have been flooded with mass tourism. Their resort is located in Icod de los Vinos, on the north coast of Tenerife, the main island, which has almost no tourism and is still very quiet and pristine. So their idea was that before they brought too much tourism, they wanted to make sure that there was a model of dong traveling and tourism and hospitality not based on exploitation and mass tourism and heavy impact on the environment. Their business is entirely open source so that other people can see that it is possible to make money operating this way. And they give access to materials that actually teach how to do it.

When I asked him about the connection back to his life as a professor at the University of Chicago (Kay was a theoretical and experimental linguist—using syntax and semantics to investigate bilingualism), he said, "Really what I use most is my training in thinking."

Working like a linguist now is about organizing thoughts and systems and problems. For Kay, running a business is like doing a PhD. And it's a very different approach from how most people—if not everyone he knows—does business. "I've never met anybody doing business who is as theoretical as I am!" But as he said, this gives a huge advantage because it leads to not being afraid of changing things that EVERYBODY takes for granted. "It's an idea, but till you get to the end, it takes a bit, right? And you change your mind and new data come in, you change your hypothesis a little bit."

He approaches running his business as a series of small-scale experiments. And I could hear the dissertation mentor as Kay walked me through the steps of his thought process: When you do research, you do it because you don't know something, right? So you try, you look at the data, you try to think about *what do I want to get? How do I want to get there?* That's your hypothesis. *And what evidence do I have that might suggest that this might work? Or won't work?* And you test it on a small scale. But crucially, you move forward.

"When we got here," Kay shared, "my wife and I both, everybody told us 'oh what you want to do is impossible! no se puede' it's impossible, it won't work!" I had to start telling people "don't say it's impossible, tell me why it's hard, or tell me what the problems will be, but you can't keep saying that it's impossible!" As Kay sees it, this mindset is something that he can trace back to his own PhD process and the years that he advised students in designing their PhD projects. There's nothing impossible. People take on the CRAZIEST topics. "You might fail but you're not afraid of them, right?" There's no such thing as "It's impossible and we just won't have an answer for this." You come up with a new answer. Simply put, PhDs reward innovation, whereas business is, "we've done it this way all our lives." Business schools train in the case study method, so students learn about all the standard problems. But, as Kay mused, learning standards is simply a matter of figuring out where to find information and reading it and thinking about it and implementing it. The harder part of a good business is thinking.

The PhD approach trains students to be innovative, and a little bit fearless. All too often, Kay sees people with a great deal of experience in business saying things like, "we've done it this way all our lives, and if it hasn't worked so far, it won't work in the future," which he sees as being very poor inductive reasoning.

As an example, one of the things they decided to do for Alberto Dorner was to try to change all the gardens from exclusively tropical to local endemic plants. And so they set up a little nursery and they experimented. Nobody had done that with the local plants, so nobody knew what could be done with them. They started studying how to replicate them, how to train them, and how to turn them into bigger shrubs. They tested things out like what happens if you water them the whole year? How much water do they take? What other plants do they grow well with? And these things cost a lot of money (you have to have someone taking care of the plant) and some of the ideas don't work. "But if you start doing this in a small nursery," he observed, "it's much cheaper, and it allows you much more experimentation than if you were to change all the villas and change all the gardens only to figure out 'oh, that didn't work!'" When you adopt an empirical mindset, mistakes, challenges, and roadblocks provide insight and new ways of doing things.

Another thing that they offer at the resort is a chef who comes into your apartment and cooks with you, teaching you to cook local food. And they used to have a high-end, top-notch professional chef, but then one day it happened that they had to have a local homemaker in to substitute. She spoke only Spanish, no English, but it worked beautifully. She was fun and she transmitted a sense of local authenticity, which as it turned out was what guests preferred. As opposed to what they had expected the guests would have wanted, now they're working with her and not with the top chef anymore. Guests can even choose to accompany her to the farmer's markets, going along to do the shopping if they want to have that experience.

Kay and I talked about the importance of building a network, and how crucial networked intelligence is in helping him prepare for the future. He mentioned having recently written a piece on LinkedIn that was getting him invited to give talks, but which is also serving to introduce him to more people who can help him tackle some of the tremendously complex, multifaceted and ever-changing nature of confronting systems-change involved in creating more sustainable business practices. He was looking forward to an upcoming meeting with a government official and former Greenpeace activist, who was going to be helping him think about how he is going to approach the international standards for assessment. Kay recognizes this as another advantage of being a scientist: "Being able to deal with complexity, being able to set aside certain things to focus on the core." For Kay, the core for the time being comprises three questions:

First, the guests:

How can we educate our guests to become better travelers?
and to know
to leave the Canary Islands knowing something beyond the experience of laying on the beach and getting a sunburn

I want them to know something about the history of our people.

The second thing is the community:

> That's the most neglected part
> People talk about the environment
> But the environment is unprotectable unless you keep in mind that there are people too
> And they deserve a decent living too
> ...
> so that's our second core project
> making sure that the community sees environmental protection as something positive
> and not as a threat to their livelihood.

And then finally, environment:

> Making sure that the oceans come back and the fish and all the seafood
> and the plankton
> and everything in the ocean can live
> and the same for the air
> and for the land
> and this is something that a lot of people are taking care of so here is where I want to piggyback
> like with the Greenpeace guy
> I want to ask him "Can you help me with this?
> Can you teach me to be more efficient so that I can focus on that part that is less known and where we have more problems, which is the community part?"

Relying on the power of his network was also something that Kay did when he was a professor:

> Networks are very important I'd say.
> I have always thought that it's crazy to think that one linguist could work better than five together
> I'm good at what I'm good at, you're good at what you're good at

You'll find your partners
And it's the same in business.

He leaves his schedule open on Fridays every week so as to be able to learn something new. Back when he was a professor, he would always make sure to attend the class of a colleague: "biology, urban architecture, African-American studies, you name it. And same is true here. I think it helps a lot." So now, on a Friday, Kay will go off exploring, perhaps he'll drive into the mountains, meet people in a neighboring village, attend a conference, anything, the only requirement being that "It has to be something not related to my job. I need to keep getting ideas from outside."

I shared with him that this same advice had been given to me by the best networker that I know, Nancy Frishberg. She shared with me that over the years it has been those meetings and conferences where you are the ONLY one thinking about language which end up being the most beneficial (for all parties involved) in the long term. Such opportunities challenge not only you to think differently, but to expand the thinking of the people you meet.

To close out our conversation, Kay shared a bit about how he gives back. He is invited to come give talks at schools and at businesses, and government agencies including a recent workshop that he gave at the cultural ministry of the secretary of government. He speaks to these groups about language and cognition, language education, language acquisition. He consults as well. He created a video series of five-minute videos to help students and their teachers and families think about all the things you are learning when you acquire a language. You don't just learn the language itself, you learn a bunch of cultural codes encoded in the ways of using the language. He's very passionate about helping support language acquisition in this way to, as he says, "give a little bit back from what I got from linguistics."

On this note of generosity, let's turn now to a researcher drawing from training in identity theory to make more room for the complexity of lived experience in work with a tribal nation. This researcher asked that we keep their name and the name of the community out of the final story that gets told, as this story becomes a reflection about storytelling more broadly, as we will soon see.

The Dynamics of Policy Development

In conversations about careers with linguists as I was developing and writing this book, I had been hearing that policy work was something that folks really wanted to know more about. And so, I actively sought out linguists with expertise in policy work. Ultimately, I found a sociolinguist who works for an Indigenous cultural organization founded in the nineteenth century, an who recently received federal core funding for its programming. This person was hired to work with them around issues of governance and to help them communicate in "funders' language"—writing up internal policy and procedures around how they work, how they resolve conflict, how they transmit knowledge (etc.).

Over the course of our conversation, we found an example of an organizational policy being created, one that struck me as the real "spark" of the story, and it formed the basis of a draft that resembled the other stories in this chapter. I shaped a story around things that I could see in this moment of work that linked back to the person's training. In this case, training in sociolinguistic variation that helped them to see policy as dynamic, varied, in flux and moving, and also identity theory that gave them the capacity to see beyond binaries and embrace a both/and approach to navigating organizational change and complexity. I also saw great skill in how this sociolinguist elicited tacit cultural knowledge to construct the policies, and then adapt and change, so that community members would see themselves reflected in the policies which became codified. I could also see how much ownership of the process this linguist was able to engender in the community. They shared with me that they had started to overhear community members explaining to one another, "Well we can do that because policy is dynamic!" The community were feeling policy's capacity for adaptability.

But then, at the stage of giving me feedback on my draft of the story, it ended up becoming apparent how much of the fabric and texture of the events described really belonged to the community and the linguist felt strongly that this was not their story to tell. We found our discussion turning then to the power one wields when taking control of a narrative—and that even when well-meaning and with all the best of intentions, a particular telling of a story can serve to erase actors whose voices were not heard, or were not centered. In this case, the particular style of storytelling I chose—giving my reader access to the here and now of someone's work, so as for her to be able to take these stories and forge connections of her own—created its own challenges, specifically that of centering me as the story collector and the linguist as agent. This concern became especially noticeable given the nature of their work with historically marginalized and racialized communities.

Thus, in telling this story, then, I return to what this linguist taught me about what they know about policy—that when done well, the community and their ways of doing things should be reflected and members should be able to recognize themselves in them. I suggest that the reader's takeaway ought to be that stories too should be tailored, they shouldn't be cookie cutter. Like good policy, stories are living, they can be changed, and they are rooted in shared meaning and value, and as someone who cares about rendering story, I care about caring for and connecting with those meanings and values.

So, as with all of the stories that I share in this book, my choice of focus—the spark, as I call it, in this case, the focus on collaboratively eliciting tacit knowledge to cocreate policy, illuminates a dynamic richness in which I see linguistic training as having enabled the capacity to hold ambiguity. And I hope that in this story about storytelling, we too were able to hold a bit more space for variety and variation, for the dynamism and vibrancy of what story form can tell us about story function, allowing for there to be room to adapt, change, and grow. And to not hold any story so closely that it can't tell us how it needs to be told.

As we come to the end of this chapter, we'll hear from Esther, who was just finishing her dissertation and thinking about "what comes next" as I started talking with her for this book.

There are many reasons that I was excited to share Esther's story. For one, I have sought to include more stories from outside the United States context, and second, I wanted to include stories from linguists working as academics in addition to those working outside the academic contexts. Having just finished and defended her dissertation, Esther is now settled firmly on an academic track, but in the course of talking to her over the course of the past couple years, I have been aware of what story researcher David Boje calls the quantum potential of her story—of the many directions her career path could have taken, and might still take. This is of course true for all of us, and so my hope in sharing a snapshot from Esther and her work during her most recent professional transition that some readers might see something of themselves and glimpse their own quantum potential.

A major part of Esther's PhD thesis directly engages with policy to critique and contest it, and so for those who want to think more about what a linguist might bring to this sphere, here's a glimpse at that work. Hopefully it sparks some ideas.

Esther Surenthiraraj

Quantum Mechanics of Storytelling

Esther's PhD thesis focuses on a community of Northern Muslims in Sri Lanka who became a community through wartime expulsion. They have lived in displacement in the north—the part of the country that Esther herself comes from—for nearly thirty years now. Esther was born into this context of war, became a migrant within Sri Lanka, and over the course of her life has moved to live in the United States and to Switzerland for her studies. Immersing herself in reading about the postwar conjuncture, she found new ways of not only making sense of her own experience of her intersecting identities of woman, migrant, a member of the Tamil ethnic group, and a Sri Lankan, but also new ways of considering what interventions the current moment might offer.

Her analysis looks at the National Policy on Durable Solutions for Conflict-Affected Displacement (NPDSCAD), exploring some of the specific ways in which the Northern Muslims are marginalized within this policy framework, and also how they contest this marginalization. Her interviews focused on themes like the meanings of home and experiences of conflict, and as they shared war-related memories, her analytical focus explored the linguistic resources they draw upon to navigate the pluralities of their experiences to contest the discursive subject position. She looked closely at referring terms that acknowledge the specific act of violence of expulsion that they have been subjected to for example, the choice between referring terms: *idampeyarkappattavarkaL* (forcibly evicted) and *idampeyarnthavarkaL* (displaced). According to her analysis "the morphological change to the root in *idampeyarkappattavarkaL* (forcibly evicted), confers a semantic shift that indicates third-party involvement which *idampeyarnthavarkaL* (displaced) does not carry" (131). With this, there is also an articulation of "the loss of choice in eviction, the violence and forcefulness of expulsion, and the loss of historical claim to residency in the North." Foregrounding an external agent in the expulsion highlights the conditions and the circumstances of the displacement, including the specific history and political conditions that mark Tamil militancy. Since this referring strategy holds a claim to return, Esther analyzes it as narrating the future in the present.

Esther is employed at the Department of English at the University of Colombo in Sri Lanka, and her PhD research at the University of Lausanne in Switzerland is hosted through a nongovernmental organization (NGO), the International Center for Ethnic Studies in Colombo. This is a research-based NGO, rather than implementation based, and when I asked Esther, she said she might be open to working in implementation one day in the distant future, but the political context has shifted in Sri Lanka, which places her now amidst a conversation about the broader meaning and purpose of education.

Sri Lanka has what they call a free education system. Undergrads enter State University through a very competitive process, and a very specific selection criteria, and receive funding by the state for their education. This is fantastic for many students who would otherwise be unable to afford tertiary education, but there is also a big state-led move to transform what some call a failed system, which is prompting discussion about what education is for. Is it about being a responsible citizen, fostering wider civic and social engagement, or is it about creating "employable" graduates? Innovative pedagogies develop people who think outside the box, thinkers who question assumptions, push boundaries, realign themselves differently in the workplace, which sets graduates to not conform to workplace norms. As policies evolve, so do practices, protocols, procedures, people and institutions who enact and embody them.

We'll close the chapter with a story within a catalyst.

A Story and a Catalyst: STAR

The STAR is a widely used model for storytelling in job interviews. Employers like Amazon tell potential employees to prepare to answer questions like "tell me about a time that you demonstrated leadership" using the structure Situation, Task, Action, and Result (Figure 5.1).

I like the model because it fits within the metaphorical domain of the constellations that we have been exploring in this book, but I also find that it is a useful way to get people thinking about the impact of their work (and by extension, the impact of their stories).

I used this activity the other day as part of a pocket-full of stories workshop. I had participants take out a piece of paper and draw four squares to develop a story about a challenge they tackled. I told them that the four-square model helps you to see what's missing, and that often with folks who have been in an academic context for a long time, we think so much about our thinking (the S, T, and A) that we can often forget the Result (R) quadrant.

I gave them an example from Katie, who had been working on a story about her work as a curriculum developer as part of a language documentation project (this is the S, the Situation of her story). Her Task was to incorporate stories from the culture into her language curriculum, but the book that she had been given as a resource was

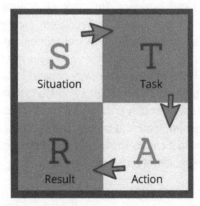

FIGURE 5.1 *STAR story model*

hard to use. There were over 700 stories and the table of contents didn't organize them by topic/theme/lesson of the story, but instead by character. Frustrated by not being able to find what she needed, Katie developed a searchable database, in which a story might have multiple tags, because it might have many different uses. This is the A of her story, the Action she took, and the first draft of her story pretty much ended there. I told the workshop participants how Katie and I brainstormed some of the various possible Rs—Results of this work that she could share when she used this story as part of a job interview. For one, this database helped her do her work better, but also, it stood to help her colleagues to do their work better, and it probably resulted in better curricula. Her database made the work easier to do, which probably ended up making it of higher quality. She might also move into the realm of the hypothetical, imagining future potential systems that she might create and how this might improve work products themselves, as well as improving collaboration and productivity.

For the stories in this book, too—I myself had to be reminded to bring forward the Results. In Kathryn's story from the last chapter for example, in the first draft, I had been so focused on describing what resources and experiences she drew on to be able to stand up that day on the bus, I entirely forgot to tell readers what happened as a result of her standing up. Thanks to the attention of my reviewers and editors, I added the detail that the man eventually quieted down, and stopped harassing the other passenger. But I take this as a reminder that our stories need listeners. To honor story listening, we need to build in some time as we are creating our stories to take some opportunities to ask our listeners how our stories are landing.

Try out this model to see whether you might need to be thinking more about the R, the results, your own impact!

If you are currently applying for jobs and are looking to use a story to help a prospective employer feel how having you around might make their lives easier, walk a story through this process. Make sure it is doing everything it can to show how you think, how you approach a problem, and especially—show the Results.

6

Navigate Your Career with WHY

I have constructed and told stories throughout the book to bring focus to what it might mean to work "like" a linguist, in each story zeroing in on an aspect of linguistic thinking as it shows up in professional or personal contexts (or both). In chasing the connections between our field of study and how this training gets expressed, I have come to have a different relationship to the phrase "I am a linguist" that has much more to do with WHY I do things the way I do them than WHERE and for WHOM I happen to do them. In sharing these stories here, I hope to inspire some thinking about your own WHYs. And, if you don't identify as a linguist, why you do what you do the way you do.

We'll start with a story from Lauren Collister, and why she went into librarianship—and in fact, she'll give us five WHYs behind that WHY. We'll hear from Jill Bishop and JPB Gerald about how the WHYs evolve, and demand re-evaluation. Charles Strauss will share a bit of the satisfaction he derives from being able to find "useful words" for his clients, and Andrea Drew about what it was like to work for the CIA and be there at critical moments when a deeper awareness of language was needed. Finally, we'll hear from Anastasia Nylund and the current crisis of imagination around work in this country and why a linguistic perspective on this issue is invaluable.

The "my story" for this chapter will feature a WHY from my life—why I chose the dissertation I did—and the catalyst will feature some ways to think about your own WHYs.

Lauren Collister

The Five WHYs

I caught up with Lauren as she was in the final stages of preparing *The Open Handbook of Linguistic Data Management* for publication. She's one of four editors, the other three linguists asked her to come on because of her knowledge of copyright and policies around data management, as Lauren calls them: "all these other kind of meta scholarship things." She couldn't hide her delight when she shared with me, "I have just loved being a co-editor on this!"

I get to read all these chapters on all these different topics
And I read every single one of these chapters with great enthusiasm
I just want to know everything about everyone's project
But I have also been doing things like checking the copyright of the figures that people are using
Making sure that they're openly licensed for use
I've been doing things with document formatting
Which is a secret thing that I really enjoy doing.

Lauren derives a great sense of satisfaction from things like making sure that the page numbers are in the right place, that all the figures are labeled appropriately, making everything look uniform, making it all fit. For her it's like wrapping a package. Document formatting is like putting the wrapping paper on nice and crisp, tying the bow, and seeing that the final product looks really nice. She also was delighted that she got to write a chapter about copyright and data, which was the entire reason she got into library work in the first place, having to do with intellectual property challenges around her own data collection with her dissertation project that a librarian helped her navigate. As she put it, "making the thing that past me needed" got her into the profession, and now she's in a position to be able to document all the things that she needed to know. "If I had had this chapter when I was a graduate student, the whole trajectory of my studies probably would have changed."

But the other thing she has been doing is helping the chapter authors understand the contract they're signing because this is an open access book. She helps them think through what it means as an author that it's going to be openly available. It's got a different kind of copyright.

She is committed to building understanding for authors that they can do more with material that gets published under an open access model than with the closed copyright model employed by for-profit academic publishers.

So, I asked Lauren more about what it really means to have a book published openly.

Turns out, it's about making things more reusable, more shareable. Giving scholarship more utility. Making it so that a reader doesn't have to pay to access it, and an author doesn't have to go through hoops to be able to share it with people. Anyone can reuse the content and build upon it. They just have to properly cite it, which after all, as Lauren says is "how science is supposed to work."

In the case of their book *The Open Handbook of Linguistic Data Management* (2021), they are working with MIT Press, and they have secured a grant to be able to offset the costs of the labor of typesetting, hosting it online, and making it openly available. These costs that typically would be put on the readers through the sales of the book now get paid ahead of time. Librarians and other people in the open space are continually looking for other business models, keeping equity front and center in their minds. As Lauren described it, librarians have a perspective, a sort of fundamental viewpoint, which is that everybody should have access to knowledge. As she put it:

> You never know what little piece of knowledge someone's
> going to get
> and do something with
> They should be able to get that!
> Whether that's you know a bit of medical information
> that can help them understand a diagnosis

or a um you know a sentence structure for a language they are
trying to learn
that suddenly of all that grammar they've been studying
makes sense!
Whether that's a pedagogical technique that helps them with their
children's homework
Whatever it is
...
They can understand the world just a little bit better
Foster curiosity
Foster learning
With a little bit of knowledge
And people should be able to access that

But living this mindset is another story. Once you start seeing how
important access to knowledge is, you get confronted with just how
much needs to be done to ensure that it happens. People deserve
to have access to knowledge, but that's not always equitable. Not
everybody can walk into a library and feel safe, not everybody can get
to a library that's near them. Not every library has the funding to buy
every book or database, whether that's a community library or a rich
university library. Not everybody reads and learns in the same way.
Working to ensure that everybody has the same level of access ends
up informing this search for a new model for publishing.

It's really complicated, because even with some of the new
models for open publishing you see the change being from paying to
read to paying to publish, which then means that fewer people can
participate in the writing and the publishing, and you're just putting
the inequity in a different bucket.

Bottom line: Open access is on the minds of lots of publishers now,
and a lot of them are having to come up with options. There are more
and more options out there, and she particularly mentioned innovative
publishers like Punctum (https://punctumbooks.com/). They have no
fees for publishing their books, and they have some radical books
on some really interesting topics that probably would never have
gotten made with the traditional models that depend on (perception
of) audience demand as the only prerequisite. And, remembering
the librarian perspective: these books will be important, interesting,

potentially life-altering to some reader. Not only is it important that the readers can access the material, here it is important that this material be "made" at all.

Lauren concluded our conversation by sharing a practice for staying engaged as a professional.

When things become stale, it's easy to lose sight and get caught up in the stressful and annoying parts that are inevitable in any job. When you find yourself asking "What is this for?" In such moments, Lauren has learned to ask herself WHY? Or more specifically a series of WHY? In her words:

> A lot of the day-to-day life of a career can be a slog
> There are infinite details and budget reports or whatever that you have to do
> And I always, when I get to that point
> ...
> "I can't handle it I don't know what's going on, I can't do this anymore"
> I sit there and I ask myself that series of why
> I ask myself why
> And I always ask myself why five times
> "Why am I in this group?"
> "Well, because my boss told me I should be in this group."
> "OK, why did my boss tell me I should be in this group?"
> "Because I have some kind of relevant experience"
> "Why do I have relevant experience?"
> "Cause I took a job years ago that taught me this."
> "Why did I take that job?"
> "Well, you know I wanted to teach online."
> "Why did I want to teach online?"
> "Cause it's the thing of the future."

At which point I chimed in to laughingly add, " ... and why do I care about the future?" And maybe that's a question better posed to you, reader!

Much appreciation and gratitude to Lauren for sharing her WHYs and for modeling this practice of the five WHYs so beautifully for us. Now, we'll turn to Charles, who began his conversation with me at a coffee shop in downtown Oakland by saying: "The thing that fascinated me more than anything else is language."

Charles Strauss

Useful Words

Linguistics is how Charles does what he does, which as he tells his clients is "to help you communicate better." Linguistics helps explain or persuade people about the merits of something, whether it be a company, idea, or name. As he explains on his website (https://straussverbal.com/): "It's my job to make sure that every sentence, every word, every letter is working hard for your business." Check out his website for stories about recent projects.

After studying linguistics at Berkeley, it was through networking with Burt Alper (fellow psycholinguist and co-founder of Catchword Naming) that Charles learned that there was a place where his love of language met his having been "raised by informercials" and his passion for adbusters. As he said, "If you despise something, you probably appreciate it on some level." His professional space is naming, marketing, and branding, where he provides services like: brand messaging, copywriting, creating names and campaigns.

He most enjoys the chance to learn, to do a deep dive about an industry, a business, a product, and then to turn that into a creative, clever piece of writing. Whatever it is that you are making: a website, a strategy, a name, Charles will give you "useful words." As he shared with me: "People might not appreciate linguistics in the business world, but they can appreciate language."

I asked Charles to share some details about his day to day. He gave an example from each of his worlds of naming and strategy. Starting with the naming work, that's "hard core thesaurus time." For a couple of weeks, he writes a ton, generating a thousand different ways to articulate the same idea. Although the end product might ultimately be one or a handful of names, the process is tremendously challenging both creatively and intellectually, and one which is best done—in Charles' experience—collaboratively, as part of a team in which everyone can bring their unique abilities. "I love creative collaboration, and since I am only comfortable working in the verbal space, I particularly enjoy getting to work with designers."

In his strategy work, it's about Interviewing people like executives, asking them about their priorities, and what they are trying to do so that he can help them articulate their vision. Because many of his clients are tech and tech-adjacent—(i.e., GE), it's often about "how can we do things faster and better." But he really enjoys learning about the industries themselves. He recently did a deep dive into maintenance on jet engines and the world of lighting for a client who was manufacturing LEDs. In a word, he enjoys nuance, and "if that's appealing to you, you might be a strategist!"

Charles also gives back to the community by volunteering his time at a school for recently arrived immigrants.

Andrea Solomon Drew

"That's It! I Am Done Reading This in English"

As a teenager, Andrea Solomon Drew went through an existentialist phase. She was reading Antoine de St. Exupéry's *Wind, Sand, and Stars* and she found that she was so taken with the power of his language that at times she had to stop reading and close her eyes to metaphorically chew and digest. She came to a sentence that stuck with her for forty years, and she recited it from memory as we talked: "Man in the presence of man is as solitary as in the face of a wide winter sky in which there sweeps, never to be tamed, a flight of trumpeting geese." That was her "That's it!" moment. She thought to herself, "I am done reading this in English! I need to hear these words in the original language." She had learned French in high school and could read it well enough to be able to appreciate its nuance.

The first thing that she discovered was that the book was called something different in French. It was *Terre des Hommes* (the land of men). She then searched for the sentence, and was humbled when she realized that it was the English translator who had created that powerful string of words. This led her to think two things: "Oh god, the power of language" and then fast upon that idea "Oh god, the power of people who can use language." In that moment, she decided to become a literary translator, and she felt the sacred nature of her responsibility to inform her work with intense study of language. She wanted to be able to render subtle differences between languages in meaning to be true to text, and to wield power with awareness of the—as she called it—the Olympian power of words. Because we use words to call things into being. As she put it:

God didn't create light,
God said "let there be light"
and the mere utterance of those words made it so.
When you are married,
you are pronounced man and wife.
The pronouncement makes it so.
And we don't enact war,
we declare war.
The declaration makes it so.

With knowledge of its enormity, Andrea committed to being a faithful steward of language. "I will translate, I will interpret, so that the real message comes through."

Years later, after she had been doing translation and interpretation for many years, she wrote to the Central Intelligence Agency (CIA), telling them that she was facile with foreign languages and that they needed to hire her. They told her that they typically like to hire people with a Master's degree, so she pursued her MA in Theoretical Linguistics at The Ohio State University. She moved to the Washington, DC area, figuring that there she would be able to find work that would enable her to express her commitment to the power of language, even if she didn't end up working at the CIA. She got a job at the Library of Congress where the critical importance of language was contained in "all the words, and all of the documents that perhaps were important to our country for centuries until now." She was just shelving books, but it didn't matter. For Andrea, it was where she wanted to be. This venue was one where language has power and demanded someone to carefully and faithfully steward and shepherd it.

Eventually she did get the gig at the CIA, and she started off as an analyst. Her job was to read foreign newspapers, snagging snippets that she thought were important things to know. This was back in the early 1980s, when not a lot of people had TVs in third-world countries, so people read newspapers, and there was a lot of important information contained within them, you could get a lot of intelligence there. Her analysis kick-started conversations, deliberations, and it required diligence and faithfulness. It required accuracy and precise knowledge.

Andrea recalled being a small child, and learning things about language in Hebrew school that she couldn't articulate until years later when she took semantics. For example, tense variation in the Bible. "Let there be light" was rendered in future tense, which means something different than past tense. She had consciousness that this meant something even then, even if she couldn't articulate it. Years later, she was able to bring this awareness, fortified with linguistic knowledge, in service to her job and the country in capturing the nuances in meaning between statements made in passive voice or in hypothetical tense. She had always noticed these things and knew them intuitively, but semantics helped her to better articulate with confidence what she was hearing to help decision-makers understand where misunderstandings could enter the scene.

When I say the world needs linguists, this is what I am talking about!!!

As she and I concluded our conversation, Andrea talked about some of the reading she is doing in her retirement. She's thinking about things like semantic shift, for example, phrases that have changed over time, such that we no longer know their origins or meaning like "sleep tight." I'll conclude this story by saying that I sleep tighter knowing there are linguists out there talking with decision-makers at critical moments. I hope it inspires some of you to bring your careful attention and nuanced understanding of language to those who really need it, precisely when and where they need it!

Jill Bishop

Making Opportunities for Linguists

We join Jill Bishop's story as she is sitting at a restaurant in Chicago doodling on a food-stained placemat. It's 2005, and she and her husband were out to dinner discussing her next career move. As she sketches out her professional past, present, and future she jots down ideas about her experiences, tracing the connections among them. What's coming to her is that she is interested in going off on her own and starting her own venture. She sees an opportunity for someone with a passion for language and culture to have an impact on companies and their multilingual employees and community members.

At that point in her professional life, she was ready to take a leap. She had a supportive partner who would help her through the transition, and she told herself: "Worst case scenario, six months later I can look back and say 'what was I thinking?' " She felt like she would be personally and professionally fulfilled and have a feeling of pride in creating something. So she embarked on a small-scale venture with limited capital, and with herself as her only employee.

Cut to 2019 when Jill and I are having our interview and Multilingual Connections is in its fourteenth year of existence and has twenty-five in-house employees, and many more linguists. "What I enjoy is giving jobs to people who love language! There aren't a lot of jobs for people like us." Of course, she also takes great pride in doing a great job for clients, helping them look good, and to accomplish their goals through translation and related services including website localization, audio transcription, subtitling, voiceover, and phone interpretation. Multilingual Connections offers these services in over seventy-five languages for clients including the City of Evanston, Northwestern University, State of Illinois, Chicago Cubs, Allstate, BP Global, Google, Airbnb, and Last Week Tonight with John Oliver.

What Jill never expected was just how much she would take to business strategy. And she is clearly good at it—evidenced by her recently being named Businessperson of the Year by the Chamber of Commerce in Evanston, IL, where her business has been headquartered since 2015. This wasn't part of the mythology about being an entrepreneur. The stories that get told tend to focus on that moment of taking a leap to start your business. The mythology centers the idea that you do it because you love what you do, but the reality is that you often stop doing what you love. The baker who opens her own shop because she loves making pie ends up spending less and less time near the oven and more time in QuickBooks managing the invoices. Luckily for Jill, she found that she really enjoys the high-level and strategic aspects of running the business, even though she didn't expect to—many people really don't handle the pressure well once the reality sets in that the job only exists only as much as you work, and that you can never really leave.

Just before starting her business, Jill had been a Culture, Diversity, and Language Consultant for the restaurant chain Chipotle—a job that enabled her to combine, as she put it, "all of the things:" Spanish teaching, English teaching, language engagement, and burritos. "I wasn't sure where it would take me, but I knew it would be something interesting!" She developed and delivered trainings, for example, teaching Spanish to restaurant managers to help them better manage multicultural teams. She also taught English to Spanish-speaking employees, having witnessed the power of language as part of a previous workplace language program for Harper College. There she saw firsthand what one class could do in terms of gaining access to functional language that could change a students' life. If she could help her students talk to their supervisors about a problem at work, or talk to their kids' teachers at school, she saw that she was doing something good and having an impact on their lives. So this is how it came to be that 1,000 Chipotle employees had her phone number.

Chipotle put her through six weeks of restaurant training, the same training that managers go through with rotations doing dishwashing, and marinating chicken, and although there were moments where she thought to herself, "Wow, I got a PhD for this?" she was grateful for the eye-opening experience of being more exhausted than she had ever been in her life, and realizing there were women who did this kind of work while eight months pregnant! As she tells it, "The most stressful moment of my career was when I was working that tortilla press. People are hungry, there's noise, it's cognitive overload—and I'm doing it in my native language. I can make small talk!" She experienced in a visceral, embodied, and unforgettable way the opportunities that being able to speak English well could afford immigrant workers, which gave her a lived sense for her business case: investing in training only pays off. Training people makes people happier, they are more engaged. It impacts the company, and impacts the customers. With even just a few hours of contact, she saw changes in morale, she saw how excited people were to bring friends and relatives to work at the company. There just were so many benefits. Employees were doing their jobs better, the customers were happier, there was less food waste, work environments were safer. She saw her part in making all of this possible, and was excited to be able to offer these kinds of services that she could see would make such an impact in so many people's lives.

This experience told her how very much language work was needed, valuable, and important, which sustained her, particularly in the early days of her company Multilingual Connections. And now, even though the company has made a shift from focusing primarily on training to translation, transcription, and research services, Jill and her employees continue making a difference in people's lives, including:

- Helping to ease the transition to living in the United States for newly resettled Farsi- and Swahili-speaking refugees by translating intake forms and materials;

- Supporting social workers, case managers, and families of abuse victims by translating case materials in several languages;

- Transcribing interviews that support government-funded research on reuniting Syrian refugee families displaced by the current crisis;

- Keeping non-English speaking employees safer on the job by translating workplace safety manuals and training modules; and

- Supporting focus group research on insomnia that could potentially lead to creation of an online therapy resource for a community of sufferers.

Feeling fortunate about the impact she has had and feeling motivated to help the next generation, Jill concluded our conversation by sharing the pitch she used to get herself in front of execs: "I would be excited to talk to you about your people, where they are from, and if there are any communication challenges." And, as she told me, "Everybody said yes! Nobody was calling and asking them these questions."

So, what questions can you get out there and start asking? What "pain points" have you identified that you know an awareness of language can ameliorate?

Most of the stories I share in this book are from linguists. Focusing the storytelling on what they do now, I draw connections back to their training. But in some cases—such as the story I am about to share from J. P. B. Gerald—the work itself is linguistic, and has connections to places where linguistic theories, frameworks, and other analytical tools stand to amplify and further the aims of the work. Ultimately, all the stories are meant to invite readers to see that their training in linguistics has cultivated helpful constructs with myriad applications for engaging in meaningful ways with the issues and challenges that speak to them.

J. P. B. Gerald

De-centering Whiteness in Foreign Language Teaching

For J. P. B. (Justin Pierce Baldwin) Gerald it was when he began teaching English in East Asia that he was confronted with linguistic imperialism. Whether or not this was explicitly recognized by his fellow teachers, what he saw was a commodification of his "native" speaker status, and an unspoken privileging of white ways of speaking. Along with the silencing of the capitalist agenda, he found an unwillingness on the part of many (if not most) of his colleagues to consider how their teaching English might be complicit with a white supremacist agenda. As a Black man, who spent most of his life in predominantly white institutions, and having been (and now continuing to be) taught almost exclusively by white educators, he found himself called to study whiteness, and specifically the perceived neutrality of professionals working in English Language Teaching, which he named the "altruistic shield."

Now as a PhD student at CUNY (City University of New York) Hunter College pursuing an EdD in Instructional Leadership, his dissertation work operationalizes language education, racism, and whiteness by focusing on this "psychological mechanism used by educators that allows [them] to outright deny or otherwise defend [them]selves from anticipated or in-the-moment accusations of racism because of what [they] consider the altruistic nature of [the] work" (2021a: 22). As the events of 2020 unfolded, this work came to have new urgency. And when, on February 18, 2020, his son Ezel was born, his scholarly work "became a moral imperative for the physical and psychological safety of his son."

In his piece, *Worth the Risk: Towards Decentering Whiteness in English Language Teaching*, Gerald offers many examples of the kinds of things that need to be changed at both the structural and personal levels if we are to decenter whiteness. He invites readers to refuse, for example, to sit on all-white academic panels, and to cite scholars of color. I think of Lauren Gawne's recent discussion of the discursive move of citation as evidential stancetaking (2021) as a way of exploring the significance of such a move through theory.

Researching J. P. B.'s recent advocacy, I want to amplify his call for the inclusion of whiteness and Critical Whiteness Studies (CWS) frameworks in teacher training, asking white educators to take a self-inventory, considering their own racial identities by doing a racial autobiography. Not only does this give them a critical lens as teachers, but it will also teach them how to teach this practice to colleagues and students, increasing salience and building capacity to address systems change. "We cannot centre the destruction and violence endemic to whiteness and show love to racialized students at the same time" (2021b: 51). I particularly enjoyed an interview he gave on The Integrated Schools podcast, the episode entitled "Checklists and Merit Badges." The idea that in approaching the work of de-centering, specifically de-centering whiteness, you find many white people asking for "the list" of things to do, terms to avoid etc., which is itself a centering move. My PIER Consulting Group business partner and I designed a training to speak directly to this in fact— we call the workshop languaging inclusion—to give a sense that this work is an ongoing process and not a static list that can be checked off, upon which completion the list do-er should then be rewarded.

Stay tuned for his book currently in development *Antisocial Language Teaching: English and the Pervasive Pathology of Whiteness*. In his words, "The book is an attempt to counterpathologize whiteness, the system that has decided who and what is ordered and disordered, and which uses language ideologies and teaching to aid in this process. To build a new version of language education, we need to dismantle whiteness within it." I very much look forward to reading it!

I hope that J. P. B.'s story sparks ideas for readers about what we linguists might bring, drawing from theoretical understandings and frameworks of how language works to further this important work of de-centering, in "making gradual, lasting progress towards the dismantling of white supremacy both in the world and, just as importantly, inside of [our]selves."

Anastasia Nylund
Thinking Bigger

I came away from my conversation with Anastasia with a sense of abundance and of great possibility. She deeply feels the importance of bringing skills and perspective to the world by radically transforming global narratives toward empathy and justice. She had recently joined Culture Hack Labs,[1] a cooperatively run consultancy focused on data-driven research and strategy services for systems change.

She finds that potential collaborators are really open to learning about what linguistics is and how a linguistic lens can help their mission. "A key skill we have as linguists is organizing and making sense of unstructured data to reveal patterns. You can sell this skill very easily by becoming familiar with some current issues the organization is working on, and demonstrating how you would contribute to solving it. Always ask yourself: 'what's the data the organization is using and how would I go about making sense of it?' "

As an example, she shared how this came to bear in a recent project for which she was researching the idea of universal basic income (UBI) for one of groups with whom she collaborates/The Rules. Despite the fact that UBI is an idea that is "unmatched in its pure potential to revolutionize our relationship with money, labor, and the future in the face of climate change" the conversation seems to be stuck among a small, closed set of participants, already familiar with and influential in defining the conversation. To help the idea achieve its potential to be a powerful tool in the struggle to change the entire logic of money, income, and wealth, the analysis done by The Rules sought to identify the cultural narratives that create and justify inequality, poverty, and ecological breakdown. They do so that they might disrupt them, and create new narrative spaces for possibility, hope, and justice.

The research began using machine learning, network analysis, and framing to understand the UBI narrative. What they found were that the frames dominating the conversation were: policy, welfare, and income only from labor, which carry negative connotations of bureaucracy, unfairness, and lack of ambition. The result therefore is that UBI stays in the grip of an old and predictable narrative: The Western narrative of capitalism as the natural global economic system. But capitalism is not the only way. We need another way because capitalism is at the root of social problems like racism (Ibram X. Kendi refers to capitalism as racism's conjoined twin in his book *How to Be An Antiracist*), and the capitalist drive is currently fueling rapacious harvesting of our natural resources, which is destroying our planet and breaking down people in the process. Since this dominant narrative has an individualistic logic, the narrative solution is to create a community-centric vision.

The dominant narrative boxes UBI in at the policy level. Thus, a new narrative poses big questions about work, creativity, and what's possible in a world where our basic needs are met just because we are alive. It's a cultural narrative of abundance.

The social media campaign they launched can be explored using the hashtag #imagineUBI—I include a social media tile here (Figure 6.1): To close our conversation, Anastasia brought the conversation back to a crisis of imagination around work. That when we ask people, "What would you do if you could do anything?" the answer is often about a particular job. But any particular job is not our work—our work is at once something broader and something much more important. The challenges currently facing our world are vast, they are far greater than traditional methods can address. What we need will be bigger than any one issue, and will likely take longer than our lifetimes to address. But the work begins today and it takes collaboration, coordination, and a complete re-examination and disruption of the cultural assumptions that undergird and reify the status quo. As they

FIGURE 6.1 *Imagine UBI social media tile (https://therules.org/)*

say at Culture Hack Labs, we need to "expose, disrupt, and shift" the ways of talking and thinking that are holding us back. To which I say again, the world needs linguists!

One of the central narratives that I have been seeking to "expose, disrupt, and shift" in this book had been the pathologizing of not knowing. One of the main reasons I wrote it, is to normalize disorientation, and this reminds me of a story.

A Story from Me: Which Diss?

My years of experience with improvisational theater tell me that a sense of not knowing is core to creativity and innovation, but it is something that we tend to pathologize as a society. In fact, it is the very reason why I chose improv for the subject of my dissertation in the first place.

I had been at that time involved in two projects that I saw as being potentially interesting and dissertation-shaped. Both were ethnographies, so I went to meet with my ethnography of communication professor, Ron Scollon. He told me that a dissertation project should represent the change that I wanted to see in the world. Project #1 was an exploration of the use of silence as a tool for expression of political dissent. It involved participant observation at a weekly vigil for peace convened on the east lawn of the capital building by the Religious Society of Friends, Quakers. I did my PhD work in Washington, DC, at the time that George W. Bush was just embarking on his "shock and awe" campaign in launching the Iraq War. I was outraged and heartbroken. I didn't recognize my country, and was in deep disalignment with the actions of my president, as I was expressing through participation in this vigil, and I suspect this was likely where Ron thought he was nudging me with the advice to look for the change I would wish to see in the world.

And yet, I could not ignore that there was something calling to me in Project #2, which involved participant observation with improvisers. In their practice, I saw a way forward. Their time together was about collaboration in community, about listening (especially when it was challenging and difficult), and more than anything, it was an immersion in practicing uncertainty and cultivating comfort with making mistakes. The very things that pursuing a doctorate—and just about every other pull of being a responsible adult—seem to be suggesting are dangerous and to be avoided at all costs. I had started doing improv almost the very first week of my doctoral program because I was having recurring nightmares that I came to understand were about teaching. I was in terror about not having all the answers. Spoiler alert: I didn't get them. The answer lay in becoming more comfortable with the not-knowing.

If there's one thing that I know, it's that not-knowing is essential.

This concept is a north star in my cosmos.

What are yours?

A Catalyst for You: Reflecting on Your WHYs

Perhaps you have read Bill Labov's (1987) "Why I Got into Linguistics, and What I Got Out of It."[2]

Spend ten minutes and take the VIA Values in Action inventory,[3] and see your top work values reflected back to you. Use these (and maybe some of the other catalysts you have done over the course of the book) to reflect on your linguistic autobiography. Which values do you see being expressed? How? Are there patterns you can discern? If so, what are they? What do you make of them? Often, your values—or what we might call your WHYs—are continually expressing themselves through you in the ways that you see things, the ways that you frame problems, the ways you work. Do you have any hobbies, art, or projects for which you volunteer your time? Do they connect? If so how?

Conclusion: Ending in the Middle

I recently attended a presentation given by linguist Jeremy Rud for NorCal Resist, an activist organization in Northern California. He was sharing some insights from sociocultural linguistics that members of the group (activists and lawyers) could bring to thinking about what it means that the US Citizenship and Immigration Services (USCIS) is planning to use AI to prescreen asylum applications. Drawing insights from a recent research project looking at algorithms and asylum, Jeremy shared insights from publicly available refugee interviews (including some produced by Oxfam, the charity) to surface issues relating to language in this context, including credibility (what gets heard as credible?), evidentiality (what counts as evidence?), and narrative (what kinds of stories seem appropriate?), that intersect with policy. The discussion was really rich and participants asked great questions.

The more he walked us through how language works in the asylum context, the more we all came to appreciate the complexity and difficultly for any human to evaluate persuasive credibility and persecution or fear of persecution considering that asylum seekers are almost always operating in a second language. They may or may not have experience working through a translator (if one is even available), and are typically unfamiliar with the genre norms and conventions of testimony. Add to this that typically the kinds of documents that decision-makers want to see are often not available in asylum situations and that typically there is little access to resources.

As a linguist, Jeremy sees the value of bringing some attention to the linguistic negotiations that are happening so that the nonprofits and advocacy groups who are supporting them can have a more nuanced appreciation of the work that story and linguistic performance are doing in these contexts.

I talked to him afterwards about this project, and his collaboration with NorCal Resist:

> I was thinking about how this organization functions as an interpreter, in many cases, between the language of this, you know, this very formalized, institutionalized immigration process on one side,
>
> right, literal policy documents on one side, and like,
>
> interactions with an incredibly diverse group of people,
>
> who in many circumstances are the most vulnerable people in our society.
>
> You know, and I am not,
>
> I don't want to victimize them.
>
> Right?
>
> They have a lot of agency in many ways.
>
> But it's, there is a linguistic process that's happening between this institution,
>
> between this system and between these individuals.

As I was listening to his NorCal Resist talk, I was thinking about the many connections I could see between Jeremy's work and that of the stories explored in this book including Marie Eve's work with refugees through Creating Puentes, Mika's reflections on AI, and Laurel's insights into credibility at the doctor's office. But then I also started seeing how this project itself embodied so many connections among Jeremy's own interests and the contexts in which he has been pursuing work. His thinking is no doubt shaped by proximity to Silicon Valley, given the location of The University of California Davis where he is currently working on his doctorate. No doubt there are other academic influences from his faculty and classmates (and from his previous mentors and colleagues at previous institutions where he studied: UC Boulder and South Dakota State). But I also see influences of his previous work experiences, which make me inclined to tell the story of how he and I know each other.

I first met Jeremy in 2016. He had just graduated with his BA in linguistics from CU Boulder and was doing a policy internship in Washington, DC. As he was thinking about his professional next steps, his professor Kira Hall encouraged him to watch a recording of a workshop that I had given a couple years before (in 2014) at CU Boulder called "Life After a Linguistics Degree." After watching it, he invited me to connect on LinkedIn and then reached out for an informational interview. I remember it being a particularly hectic time when he reached out and although I didn't respond quickly, Jeremy was gently persistent, which I suggest as a model for readers of this book.

Eventually we did find a time to meet, and we talked about the advocacy world and how my team—the Research Interpretation and Application (RIA) team at FrameWorks—works with advocates to apply research-generated communications insights and strategy. We talked about the various issue areas that he had been working in through his work with the Joint National Committee for Languages—National Council for Languages and International Studies, including education, international relations, and technology and what he was learning about language policy and policy analysis.

We stayed in touch and a few months later, Jeremy took an opportunity to work as a Spanish instructor at his alma mater, South Dakota State University. After being there just one semester, he figured out how to get budget from the university for an invited speaker, and he flew me out to give a series of workshops. As part of my visit, he organized lunch and dinner meetings with members of the faculty and staff, guest lectures in several classes in the department, he got me an interview on the local public radio station, and as part of the main event—an evening workshop—Jeremy also hosted a networking mixer to which he invited local employers, recent alum, and a photographer to take professional headshots for participants. It was amazing, and I got a sense for his energy, dedication, sense of purpose, and commitment to the work of career development and professionalization of members of our field.

After three years, he moved to California to pursue his PhD, where we pick up with this project on AI and asylum, which may end up becoming a part of his dissertation, and now hopefully you readers are starting to see many of the connections that I do: his interests in advocacy and language advocacy specifically; his gifts as a teacher and his passion for building community and giving back to community; his orientation to application, dissemination, and impact. These shape and guide and inform his interests as a linguist, and his abilities as a linguist contribute to these areas in turn.

I hope you can also start to see the impact of his work as you envision him giving his talk for NorCal Resist and as you hear him talk about the genre conventions for stories in this domain—what asylum seekers need to do with language in their stories to make them sound credible—and hopefully you too can see the energy in this moment and perhaps feel just how much the world needs this bright light. To extend the metaphor, you might also be seeing a bit more about how this star forms a constellation.

If I were to have included Jeremy's story in the body of the book, I might have picked the linguistic performance of credibility as a spark to build a story around. And then, as I just described, there are myriad potential connections which I might have used to build a link back to something from his background and experience. But I hope you are now also starting to see how these links work, and maybe you drew some of your own. Links work in all directions—past, present, and future and within and across stories.

I included Jeremy's story here in the Conclusion to end with someone smack dab in the middle of their story, because that's where I'm imagining you are as you read this book. You have an interest in linguistics as a bright spot, what others did you discover as you read this book? What more will you find as you speak to the people for whom this book has sparked a desire to reach out. I encourage you to bring listening to these sparks as you listen to yourself talk about the things that light you up and point you forward, because the world needs all your bright sparks!

While it can be easy to have a scarcity mindset about work, one of the things that stories DO is foster abundance. After listening to nearly forty stories now from linguists with a variety of academic specializations, with varied levels of training, at different stages of their careers, and from different professional sectors (both academic and beyond), those who currently think of themselves as linguists, those who don't, those who work as part of organizations (large and small, for-profit and not-for-profit), and those who are entrepreneurs, I hope that you have glimpsed some possibilities that you had not yet thought of, and that you are feeling a sense of possibility.

I also hope the book has prompted more questions than answers. I hope it has inspired you to find your own set of people that you want to get out there and elicit stories from, and to share your stories with.

As I was thinking about the best way to end this book, I decided that I would convene a conversation for folks whose stories were in the book. I thought I might give them a chance to meet one another and to hear one another's stories, since most of them don't know one another. Presented with an opportunity to tell their story again—and in some cases years later—introduced some interesting variation. Some folks talked about the experience of sharing their story, rather than retelling it. Others reflected on the big ideas, introducing some new ways of understanding who they are and what they do, Kathryn for example, who shared reflections on using mixed quantitative and qualitative approaches in her work in the healthcare communication sector said:

> I always laugh frankly, at the idea of a data scientist
> as if there's like a scientist who doesn't deal with data.
> That's kind of like my little pet peeve of terminology.
> But I am frequently asked to speak on like behalf of data science,
> or speak to data science.
> And I do always try to remind folks that social science is part of data science,
> and that there's room for us there.

I knew that I would hear about change. As a linguist, I feel strongly about modeling an openness to change, even though as an author, it is tempting to wish that stories would stay put. Truth is, of course, that we are all always changing. Our world is always changing. It stands to reason that our work—not to mention our relationship to our work—is always going to be changing. Several people have changed jobs since I wrote their stories for this book.

A theme that I did not expect was that of privilege. That for some of these folks, being in academia felt like being surrounded by people in privilege and that staying in academia would have meant training people who were already privileged, when there was a calling to share knowledge more widely and with those who might otherwise not have access to it.

There was also much talk about identity, and much talk about feeling a sense of a split identity, as exemplified by one participant who shared that while her training in linguistics, in her words, "seamlessly" prepared her for the professional role, it was a very difficult transition because she had spent ten years preparing to be a professor, and that was the only thing she wanted to do.

> So the teaching and the research and all of the stuff that just I was so passionate about,
> I was ready for,
> and it just didn't work out.
> And personal reasons and confluence of a variety of factors, I had to pivot and I had to pivot hard.
> And I was like, "I don't even know what to pivot to."

Readers may have noticed that I have largely avoided the topic of identity in this book. In more than a decade now of having conversations with linguists who work in contexts beyond the academic, I often hear that people no longer consider themselves linguists, or as one participant in the focus group shared, there can be a sense of "coming back to it"—in this case when asked to serve on a committee with the Linguistics Society of America's Special Interest Group for Linguistics Beyond Academia.

I decided long ago that it is not for me to label anyone, or to say how anyone should be orienting to the identity term "linguist," but for my part, I have never stopped using the term because of the expansive view I have chosen to adopt of the field and its potential applications.

And, I have of course run into my share of gatekeepers, people telling me that "this" is linguistics and "that" over there isn't. But I personally find it much more valuable to ask "what if?" or "how might we?"—design-thinking kinds of questions. What if a person's having studied linguists gives them some helpful ways of approaching work tasks? What might that look like? How might we help share this in ways that help others be similarly inclined to look for possibilities?

All of this is not to say that there was not grief and loss. I experienced—and still experience more than a dozen years after receiving my PhD, and now more than seven years working outside of an academic institution—profoundly painful moments, and very real financial implications that I will be living with for the rest of my life.

I won't dwell on it, but websites like RIP my academic career https://rip-my-academic-career.decasia.org/, Versatile PhD, and Linguists Outside Academia speak to the grief, loss, and sense of isolation that this transition can engender when one moves from a highly organized space to one where there is little structure and even less support.

These conditions are truly unfortunate.

And they are often compounded by unhelpful attitudes, willful ignorance, and unrealistic expectations imposed on the people trying to survive them. While I know that one book is not going to change the conditions, what I hope it can do is offer a sense that it is real, this shock to the system that you are feeling. That you are not alone, and that the world needs you.

If you are currently navigating this transition, know you are not alone, seek out community—find (and build) connections. If you have been through it, and now find that you have some perspective to offer, find ways to share your story.

I'm always looking to share career stories, as is Gretchen McCulloch on All Things Linguistic, Lauren Gawne on Superlinguo, and Hannah Van Brundt at Linguamonium.

Don't forget the Linguistics Society of America's Linguistics Beyond Academia (LBA), Special Interest Group (SIG).

If you know someone who is charting their career, be curious with them.

Bring an attitude of "how might we?"

Even if—ESPECIALLY IF—you are their academic advisor.

You don't have to have all the answers. The best thing you can do is support the exploration. Use the work interrogatives: the WHO, WHAT, WHEN, WHERE, WHY, and HOW to be reflective about work. Especially WHY.

I'll close with a recollection from the time I was interviewing to work at the US Census. I had talked to several friends who worked there, and in hindsight, I realize that I asked lots of questions about the WHAT and HOW of the work, but very few about the WHY. And as it turned out, the interview itself really focused on the WHY of the work. Many people who have devoted their professional lives to working at the Census or other Federal Agencies do so because they believe in the ability of government to make a difference. The Census, for example supports "planning and funding for health clinics and highways, fire departments and disaster response, education programs such as Head Start and college tuition assistance, and so much more" (Maryland Department of Planning).

I'm very grateful that I started chatting with the person next to me on the Metro on my way out to Suitland, MD, for my job interview that day. I guess I looked nervous and was not used to wearing a suit. Who knows why we struck up a conversation, but I'm glad we did, because she asked me, "Isn't it amazing when you think about it?" and as we sat there together, she made me think about the Census. It was started by Thomas Jefferson. It's a massive undertaking. With a long and rich history. The work involves thousands of people (and even that day on the Metro, hundreds of folks heading with me across the Potomac) to make it happen, to interpret and disseminate the information. It really is amazing when you think about it!

Of course the folks who I then interviewed with—the folks who actually make the questions—really do feel like they go to work every day in "the room where it happens." As part of my job interview, my would-be supervisor showed me the two questions which had changed because of his decades of work. Each was a change of just a couple of words, but these words had to do with how we talk about race and racial identity and language use at home. Because I showed appropriate enthusiasm and had been primed to think in ways that prompted questions that satisfied him, he produced the many binders which contained the formidable work involved in making those apparently small changes happen.

In so many ways, the decanal Census sets the tone for national conversations about things like how we live as families and communities and what we need to flourish, and I'm so glad that I stopped to be curious about that.

One of the things that has been the most fun for me in writing this book is finding a sense of wonder in the connections: what are the odds that I would talk to a hotelier and a user researcher who talks to hoteliers? I simply adored learning more about the Wikimedia Foundation—their organizational structure and ethos—and then being able to put that knowledge together with my conversation with Lauren about open and Laura about information preservation and storage. Like the Census, I had only really thought about Wikipedia from the perspective of user, and I was grateful to be be afforded some perspective on its societal significance. Or the conversation with Anastasia about what taking an anti-capitalist stance really means and what rules need to be changed. And how we might do that.

But the biggest difference has been that writing this book changed my relationship with my own voice. I have often heard that my writing style is "informal" and "conversational" but one of the reviewers of this book went so far as to describe my writing style as "chatty" and say that my tendency to at times be "poetic" would make my message inaccessible and off-putting to many readers, especially to men. I revisited Kathryn Campbell-Kibler's excellent (2006) resource *Why Don't They Hear What I Say?* about gender ideology and erasure and relationships to power. I took refuge in knowing that readers of drafts of this book told me that it gave them hope, that they feel empowered and agentive. I believe the style has a role to play in inviting readers in. You may notice that I have doubled-down on this style here in the conclusion. I will not doubt its utility.

What in your own professional life could benefit from taking a moment to ask "why?" or "why not?" In *Bringing Linguistics to Work*, I talked a great deal about how an improv mindset shaped my approach. The writing of the book prompted me to go back into the history of improv to find that there are three women at the heart of the genesis of this art form and practice, whose stories have been erased. Whose voices are being silenced in your world of work? Whose voices could you be amplifying? How would that change how you understand what you do? How would that change how you do what you do?

I hope that reading, reflecting on, and discussing these stories has inspired you to pay more attention to opportunities for sharing stories, moments for eliciting them, and for using them to bring focus to skills and abilities. I hope that by honoring the transformative work that such talk can do, you invest the required patience and make the choice to trust and support others.

And now that you have started cultivating a story-listening practice, keep a notebook and jot down fleeting observations that might come up as you are reading reports and articles, or as you are posting or responding to a post. Pay particular attention to things that register as frustration ("I wouldn't have done it that way!") or as admiration ("I never even thought of applying that approach to this kind of a problem"). These flashes of insight speak to your unique differentiators. They are telling you something about what makes you come alive. About your sparks. Capture them. Bring these to networking events and informational interviews to share with your professional network. Where do they see opportunities for using your WHATs and HOWs to best solve the WHYs that speak to you?

Finally, I hope that the book has started giving you some momentum.

What comes next?

Do one small thing!

As just one example: I often get asked whether or not someone should mention the term "linguistics," and/or if you have a PhD when or whether and where to say so. People share advice that they have been given to definitely do or definitely don't do one or the other because people on the hiring end of things may not understand or may bring prejudicial thinking to evaluate their candidacy. And I have been in the position where someone has projected their assumptions about PhDs on to me: that I won't be able to work as part of a team, that I won't be able to work fast enough, that I won't like not being able to independently direct and select my projects.

My inclination is to move toward being able to talk about both of these things with more people more of the time eventually.

But that probably won't be where we start.

Start with one small thing.

Try calling yourself a linguist, or try not doing so.

Listen to the response.

None of us can singlehandedly dismantle systemic inequity, and we can't do it all at once, and probably not in a networking event, but we can start. We can be mindful of one small choice that we make in an interaction that is done purposefully and with intention to change the conversation.

And it might be uncomfortable.

But our own comfort is probably not the right measure of success.

Maybe you will choose to explain why a linguistics approach is valuable.

Maybe you will use a technical term.

Maybe you will look for the next opportunity.

What's important is that you recognize that you have choices.

And down the road, when you have more power and influence, be a part of the change—like Jill, whose story we heard earlier—for whom one of the most motivating things about her business, Multilingual Connections, is that she can use any success to hire more linguists!

Keep asking these questions! How can you change systems?

Especially WHY.

And then ask it again.

And again.

Finally, give yourself some structure.

For me, that means seeking out two career conversations a week and two meetings (networking events or conferences) a month. *In Designing Your Life* the authors give a formula that for every twenty-five conversations you have, you will unearth an opportunity. Following this formula, two conversations a week and two meetings a month would stand to generate about five opportunities a year, which seems to be about right: One for you, four for your community.

Because the world needs us.

Here's to what comes next!

APPENDICES

Appendix 1: The Work Interrogatives

Use these to reflect on where you have been, where you are, and where you're going.

WHY
The problem you wish to solve

WHAT
Skills you bring

HOW
Your approach

WHO
For and with WHO(M) do you wish to work, and who can you be at work?

WHERE
Do you have geographical constraints or preferences? Do you want to work in an office?

WHEN
Are you looking for a set schedule or flexibility/full-time or part-time?

WHY
Salary, benefits, lifestyle implications of the work.

The work interrogatives can be used to structure a systematic and rigorous thinking-through a linguist's relationship to her work. WHAT tends to be where conversations about career typically seem to start ... but unfortunately often end: "I just want to do linguistics!" The problem is that as conceptualized, this WHAT is not fine-grained enough to be useful or actionable. The good news is that the tools of WHY and HOW, together with reflection on WHAT can help linguists arrive at a much more fine-grained understanding of what you are after when it comes to the day-to-day details of work tasks. How exactly are you planning to use your linguistics? Why this skill and not that one? Why this domain instead of a different one?

And perhaps it bears mentioning here that this reflection can only really be about where (and when) you are at currently. Priorities shift, and experiences and opportunities necessarily shape and redirect trajectories. Spending an hour (or more) a week on LinkedIn can be a great way to make some time and space to reflect and take stock: Where am I now? Where have I been and where am I heading?

WHO contains worlds, and is often absent from many first-time job seekers' conversations about work. Luckily, informational interviews are great sources of rich information about WHOs. WHO might be relevant in terms of colleagues and respective roles (who manages, oversees, provides feedback on whose ideas and how). Or it might be who you will work for, which might include the work sector or industry, a specific organization, or even a team or a manager. Who are your clients? How much client contact will you have? How much do you want? Do you want to work for yourself? No matter what arrangement you decide might suit you, it will also bear thinking about who you will be at work. Some people want to bring as much of themselves as possible to work, others may purposefully design their work lives so that only certain parts of their identities are expressed. Sometimes this is owing to the workplace culture.

WHERE and WHEN remind us to pay attention to the contexts in which we work, and also to the opportunities which surround us.

Finally, we come back to WHY, and this time it is your WHY—why you work, including your workstyle preferences, your professional goals—and these may well change over time. There are many tests out there that help you take stock of your **workstyle preferences** and these are typically time well spent. If you are currently a student, you might be able to get many of them for free. Find out from your career center whether you have access to the Strong Skills Inventory, and crucially whether you have access to a person who has been certified to facilitate the debrief with you. If not, not to worry, there are plenty available online—and you can always think about hiring a career coach. I take stock of my workstyle preferences at any chance I get because they often change: I always learn something new about how I work, and what contexts and factors don't support my best work.

Appendix 2: Conversation with a Job Ad: The WHAT, HOW, and WHY

WHAT will you be asked to do? (motivate your decision about how to rank top three)
1.
2.
3.

HOW do they want it be done? (i.e., collaboratively, using particular technologies, etc.)
1.
2.
3.

WHY does this work matter (What do they say about why it's important? What's at stake?)
1.
2.
3.

Appendix 3: List of Stories in the Book

S. No.	Ch.	Story	Linguistic Concept/ Feature	What this person does now
1	1	Charlotte Linde	Exemplars	Independent scholar, Anthropology of Wisdom research project
2	1	Samantha Beaver	Speech act theory	Linguist, Memra Language Services
3	1	Anne Charity Hudley	Fostering a more inclusive linguistics	Professor of Education, Stanford University
4	2	Carolyn	Business	Researcher, Comcast
5	2	Renee	Business	Professional athlete

S. No.	Ch.	Story	Linguistic Concept/ Feature	What this person does now
6	2	Matt	Business	Proposal writer
7	2	Holly	Research	PhD student, Indiana University Bloomington
8	2	Steven	Innovation	Social change advocacy focusing on language use and engagement
9	2	Zara	Government	Translation and intercultural communication
10	2	Kathryn	Healthcare (Communication)	Research Director at InVibe Labs
11	2	Elvira	Tech	Google (formerly)
12	2	Elizabeth	Education	Community College Instructor
13	2	Hollis	Nonprofit	Contract writer at George Kaiser Family Foundation and Director at Thread Strategies
14	3	Didem Ikizoğlu	The meaning of giving methodological detail	Language expert, Nuance Communication
15	3	Abby Bajuniemi	Research granularity comparison to variation	UX researcher and designer
16	3	Greg Bennett	Adjacency Pairs Self-advocacy at work	Conversation Designer, Salesforce
17	3	Janneke Van Hofwegen	Research findings: ("outcomes" in the language of UX) and the ability to effectively communicate them	UX researcher in Silicon Valley

S. No.	Ch.	Story	Linguistic Concept/ Feature	What this person does now
18	3	Eli Asikin-Garmager	Research process—collaboration	Design Research, Wikimedia Foundation
19	3	Anthony Koth	Semantic analyses—cluster analysis	Taxonomist, Indeed
20	4	Laura Welcher	Preserving not just information (language) but meaning	Director of Operations, Long Now Foundation
21	4	Kathryn Campbell-Kibler	Bystander activism on the bus	Professor, Ohio State University
22	4	Serena Williams	Genealogy is about now	Founder, Chronos Heritage Services
23	4	Laurel Sutton	Advocating at the doctor	Strategist and Linguist, Sutton Strategy Catchword Naming
24	4	Mackenzie Price	Questions that don't get asked at work	Editorial Advisor, Diversity + Inclusion, Dotdash
25	4	Marie-Ève Monette	Structural humility	Director, Creating Puentes (language access)
26	5	Mika Hama	Listening	Director of Strategy and Innovation, Second Language Testing, Inc.
27	5	Serena P.	Words to keywords	Digital Marketing Manager at an e-commerce company
28	5	Kólá Túbòsún	Diacritics	Founder and creator of YorubaName.com and Lexicographical advisor and consultant

S. No.	Ch.	Story	Linguistic Concept/ Feature	What this person does now
29	5	Kay Gonzales	Running a business is like a dissertation project	Co-owner of Alberto Dorner resort
30	5	Sociolinguist	Co-creating organizational policy that dynamically reflects community	Strategy and development manager at a community organization
31	5	Esther Surenthiraraj	Policy analysis	Lecturer, Department of English, Faculty of Arts, University of Colombo
32	6	Lauren Collister	Open access	Director of the Office of Scholarly Communication and Publishing, University of Pittsburgh Library System
33	6	Charles Strauss	"useful words"	Senior Brand Copywriter, Corelight Inc.
34	6	Andrea Solomon Drew	Exuberances and deficiencies of translation	Central Intelligence Agency (CIA) ret.
35	6	Jill Bishop	Localization and Translation	Founder and CEO, Multilingual Connections
36	6	J. P. B. Gerald	De-centering whiteness	EdD student in Instructional Leadership, City University, New York
37	6	Anastasia Nylund	Narrative analysis to promote empathy and justice	Researcher, project manager, and creator of order in chaotic data, Culture Hack Labs
38	7	Jeremy Rud	Narrating credibility	Sociocultural Linguist and PhD student, University of California, Davis

Notes

1 RECKONING WITH YOUR INTENTIONS

1 I attribute the term "noisy not" to Charlotte, but over the course of more than a decade's worth of conversations with her, it appears to have been my adaptation of her term "noisy silence." Charlotte tells me that she is happy for me to use "noisy not" as a "result of some kind of strange mind meld in our conversation," which strikes me as just perfect!!

3 HOW LINGUISTS BRIGHTEN

1 If you identify as someone who likes to play with language, you might appreciate Joe Coleman's website design. As Eli shared, "Joe sort of straddles UX Writing and more traditional marketing copywriting (not sure how he self-identifies, we've never met), but his website sure is fun to play with!"

5 BRIGHTEN AROUND THE WORLD

1 As a digital marketer you will also need to be always updated on new features and releases, which is why you will find a lot of communities and useful resources online. A few that she recommends are: searchengineland.com, marketingland.com, and https://blog.google/products/ads-commerce/.

2 Although Twitter had publicly announced in 2014 its intention to add Yorùbá to the list of languages into which the platform was being translated, and had opened the translation platform to translators interested in helping with the localization, the whole translation project was shut down a few months later, and Twitter has remained only in English and a handful of other languages (Túbòsún P.C.).

6 NAVIGATE YOUR CAREER WITH WHY

1 https://www.culturehack.io/.
2 https://www.ling.upenn.edu/~wlabov/Howlgot.html.
3 https://www.viacharacter.org/.

References

"Alberto Dorner Boutique & Luxury Lodging," https://albertodorner.com/ (accessed July 13, 2020).

Bajuniemi, A. (n.d.), "Abby Bajuniemi, PhD: Research & Design, Strategy, & Speaking," https://www.abajuniemi.com (accessed March 3, 2020).

Bennett, G. (2018) "Conversational Style: Beyond the Nuts and Bolts of Conversation," in R. J. Moore, M. H. Syzmanski, R. Aran, and G. J. Ren (eds.), *Studies in Conversational UX Design*, pp. 161–80, Cham: Springer.

Berez-Kroker, A., B. McDonnell, E. Koller, and L. Collister (eds.) in press. *The Open Handbook of Linguistic Data Management*, Cambridge, MA: MIT Press.

Bolles, R. N. (2019) *What Color is Your Parachute: A Practical Manual for Job-Hunters and Career-Changers*, New York: Ten Speed Press.

Botsociety (May 8, 2020) Applying Linguistics to Conversational Design: Greg Bennett from Salesforce [Video], YouTube, https://www.youtube.com/watch?v=6PTCv_r6NVY(accessed September 13, 2021).

Briller, S. B., and A. Goldmacher (2009) *Designing an Anthropology Career*, Lanham, MD: AltaMira.

Bucholtz, M., A. C. Liang, and L. A. Sutton (eds.) (1999) *Reinventing Identities: The Gendered Self in Discourse*, Oxford: Oxford University Press.

Campbell-Kibler, K. (2006) "Why Don't They Hear What I Say?," *Fairer Science*. Available online: http://www.fairerscience.org/dr_x.html (accessed July 8, 2020).

Challenge others to take the Census today. Maryland Department of Planning. Available online: https://content.govdelivery.com/accounts/MDMDP/bulletins/298b84d (accessed July 5, 2021).

Charity Hudley, A. H., (2018), "Engaging and Supporting Undergraduate Students in Linguistics Research and Across the University," *Journal of English Linguistics*, 46 (3): 199–214. Available online: https://doi.org/10.1177/0075424218783445(accessed September 13, 2021).

Charity Hudley, A. H., C. L. Dickter, and H. A. Franz (2017) *The Indispensable Guide to Undergraduate Research: Success in and Beyond College*, New York: Teachers College.

Charity Hudley, A. H., and C. Mallinson (2018) "Dismantling 'The Master's Tools': Moving Students' Rights to Their Own Language from Theory to Practice," *American Speech*, 93 (3–4): 513–37. doi:10.1215/00031283-7271305.

Charity Hudley, A. H., and C. Mallinson (2018) "Introduction: Language and Social Justice in Higher Education," *Journal of English Linguistics*, 46 (3): 175–85. doi:10.1177/0075424218783247 (accessed September 13, 2021).

Charity Hudley, A. H., C. Mallinson, and M. Bucholtz (2020) "Toward Racial Justice in Linguistics: Interdisciplinary Insights into Theorizing Race in the Discipline and Diversifying the Profession," *Language*, 96 (4): 200–35. doi:10.1353/land.2020.0074.

Charity Hudley, A. H., C. Mallinson, M. Bucholtz, N. Flores, N. Holliday, E. Chun, and A. Spears (2018) "Linguistics and Race: An Interdisciplinary Approach towards an LSA Statement on Race," Proceedings of the Linguistics Society of America, 3 (8): 1–14. http://dx.doi.org/10.3765/plsa.v3i1.4303 (accessed September 13, 2021).

Charity Hudley, A. H., C. Mallinson, M. Bucholtz, N. Flores, N. Holliday, E. Chun, and A. Spears (2019) "LSA Statement on Race," *Linguistics Society of America*, May. Available online: https://www.linguisticsociety.org/content/lsa-statement-race (accessed June 2020).

"Charrette," https://en.wikipedia.org/wiki/Charrette (accessed April 30, 2020).

Coleman, J. (n.d.) "Joe Coleman, https://getcoleman.com (accessed March 20, 2021).

Content Translation," https://www.mediawiki.org/wiki/Content_translation (accessed April 30, 2020).

Cooke, R. (2020) "Wikipedia Is the Last Best Place on the Internet," *Wired*, 17 February. Available online: https://www.wired.com/story/wikipedia-online-encyclopedia-best-place-internet/ (accessed March 30, 2021).

Cullen, M. (2008) *35 Dumb Things Well-Intentioned People Say*, Garden City, NY: Morgan James.

Dicks, M. (2018) *Storyworthy: Engage, Teach, Persuade, and Change Your Life through the Power of Storytelling*, Novato, CA: New World Library.

Dweck, C. S. (2007) *Mindset: The New Psychology of Success*, New York: Ballantine.

Erard, M. (2012) *Babel No More: The Search for the World's Most Extraordinary Language Learners*, New York: Free Press.

Gal, S. (1978) "Peasant Men Can't Get Wives: Language Change and Sex Roles in a Bilingual Community," *Language in Society*, 7

(1): 1–16. *JSTOR*, Available online: www.jstor.org/stable/4166971 (accessed March 8, 2021).

Gawne, L. (2021) "The Linguistics of Hyperlinks," *Superlinguo*. Available online: https://www.superlinguo.com/post/643129872157491200/the-linguistics-of-hyperlinks (accessed March 9, 2021).

Gerald, J. P. B. (2020a) "Worth the Risk: Towards Decentering Whiteness in English Language Teaching," *BC TEAL Journal*, 5 (1): 44–54. https://doi.org/10.14288/bctj.v5i1.345.

Gerald, J. P. B. (2020b) "Combatting the altruistic shield in English language teaching," *NYS TESOL Journal*, 7 (1): 22–5. Available online: http://journal.nystesol.org/jan2020/3_AP.pdf (accessed March 8, 2021).

Gerald, J. P. B. (n.d.) "JPB Gerald: The Professional Home for JPB Gerald's Public Work," https://jpbgerald.com (accessed March 9, 2021).

Gladwell, M. (2005) *Blink: The Power of Thinking without Thinking*, New York: Little, Brown and Company.

Goguen, J., C. Linde, and M. Murphey (1986) "Crew Communications as a Factor in Aviation Accidents," *NASA Technical Memorandum 88254*. Available online: https://www.researchgate.net/publication/23588590_Crew_communication_as_a_factor_in_aviation_accidents (accessed March 30, 2021).

Gonick, L., and T. Kasser (2018) *Hyper-Capitalism: The Modern Economy, It's Values, and How to Change Them*, New York: The New Press.

Goodwin, C. (1994) "Professional Vision," *American Anthropologist*, 96 (3): 606–33. Available online: www.jstor.org/stable/682303 (accessed March 8, 2021).

Grant, A. (2014) *Give and Take: Why Helping Others Drives Our Success*, New York: Viking.

Grant, A. (2016) *Originals: How Non-Conformists Move the World*, New York: Viking.

Grant, A. (2021) *Think Again: The Power of Knowing What You Don't Know*, New York: Viking.

Harley, A. (2015) "Personas Make Users Memorable for Product Team Members," *Nielsen Normal Group*, 16 February. Available online: https://www.nngroup.com/articles/persona/?lm=why-personas-fail&pt=youtubevideo (accessed March 7, 2021).

Heritage, J., and G. Raymond (2005) "The Terms of Agreement: Indexing Epistemic Authority and Subordination in Talk-in-Interaction," *Social Psychology Quarterly*, 68 (1): 15–38.

Holmberg, C., and J. Muwwakkil (2020) "Conversation in the classroom," *Phi Delta Kappan*, 101 (5): 25–9. doi:10.1177/0031721720903824 (accessed September 13, 2021).

"How I Built This with Guy Raz" (2020) [Radio] NPR, 3 February. Available online: https://www.npr.org/2020/01/31/801648253/m-m-lafleur-sarah-lafleur (accessed February 5, 2020).

Kazeem, Y. (2019) "How Google Created a Nigerian Voice and Accent for Maps," *Quartz Africa*, 30 July. Available online: https://qz.com/africa/1673615/how-googles-nigerian-voice-accent-was-created/ (accessed March 8, 2021).

Kazeem, Y. (2020) "These Are the Nigerian English Words Added to the Oxford Dictionary," *Quartz Africa*, 23 January. Available online: https://qz.com/africa/1789168/nigerian-english-words-added-to-oxford-dictionary/ (accessed March 8, 2021).

Kemp, A. (2016) *Say the Wrong Thing*, Lancaster: Joy Will Come.

Kendi, I. X. (2019) *How to Be an Antiracist*, New York: One World.

Keshtcher, Y. (2021) "What Does a UX Writer Actually Do?," *Career Foundry*, 7 January. Available online: https://careerfoundry.com/en/blog/ux-design/ux-writing-what-does-a-ux-writer-actually-do/ (accessed March 7, 2021).

Kho, N. (2019) *The Thank-You Project: Cultivating Happiness One Letter of Gratitude at a Time*, New York: Running Press.

"Language & Culture: Language Variation in the Classroom," https://www.doe.virginia.gov/instruction/english/literacy/language_culture.shtml(accessed September 13, 2021).

"The Language of Science and the Science of Language: Buckeye Language Network Summer Research Program," https://u.osu.edu/blnsummer/(accessed September 13, 2021).

Leary, J. P. (2018) *Keywords: The New Language of Capitalism*, Chicago: Haymarket Books.

Lefkowits, A. (Producer) (August 19, 2020) "Checklists and Merit Badges: JPB Gerald on Whiteness" [Audio Podcast]. https://integratedschools.org/podcast/jpbgerald/.

Linde, C. (2020) "Social Construction of Wisdom in Institutions," in P. Kao and J. Alter (eds.), *Capturing the Ineffable: An Anthropology of Wisdom*, 122–52, Toronto: University of Toronto Press.

"The Long Now Foundation," https://longnow.org/people/board/sb1/ (accessed April 30, 2020).

Montel, A. (2019) *Wordslut: A Feminist Guide to Taking Back the English Language*, New York: Harperwave.

Oluwafemi, B. (2014) "It Took Only Two Years, but Twitter Is Finally Getting Translated into Yoruba," *techcabal*, 14 November. Available online: https://techcabal.com/2014/11/14/twitter-yoruba/ (accessed May 25, 2020).

Pink, D. H. (2002) *Free Agent Nation: The Future of Working for Yourself*, New York: Warner Business.

Podesva, R. Personal Communication.

Price, M. (2017) *Power through Participation: A Sociolinguistic Approach to Identifying Leadership in Executive Education Classroom Discourse*, PhD diss., Georgetown University Graduate School of Arts and Sciences, Washington, D.C.

Raymond, G., and J. Heritage (2006) "The Epistemics of Social Relations: Owning Grandchildren," *Language in Society*, 35: 677–705.

Rickford, J. R., and R. J. Rickford (2000) *Spoken Soul: The Story of Black English*, New York: Wiley.

"The Rosetta Project," http://rosettaproject.org/ (accessed April 30, 2020).

Salazar, K. (2018) "Why Personas Fail," *Nielsen Normal Group*, 28 January. Available online: https://www.nngroup.com/articles/why-personas-fail/ (accessed March 7, 2021).

Seib, P. (2010) "Africom's Impressive Public Diplomacy Product," *USC Center on Public Diplomacy Blog*, 7 August. Available online: https://uscpublicdiplomacy.org/blog/africom's-impressive-public-diplomacy-product (accessed March 8, 2021).

Sinek, S. (2011) *Start with Why: How Great Leaders Inspire Everyone to Take Action*, New York: Portfolio.

Slim, P. (2009) *Escape from Cubicle Nation: From Corporate Prisoner to Thriving Entrepreneur*, New York: Portfolio.

Surenthiraraj, E., and N. De Mel (2019) " 'Two Homes, Refugees in Both': Contesting Frameworks – The Case of the Northern Muslims of Sri Lanka," *Journal of Social and Political Psychology*, 7 (2): 1044–64. https://doi.org/10.5964/japp.v7i2.850.

The Story of Stuff Project (July 16, 2012) The Story of Change [Video], The Story of Stuff Project, https://www.storyofstuff.org/movies/story-of-change/(accessed September 13, 2021).

The Story of Stuff Project (October 1, 2013) The Story of Solutions [Video], The Story of Stuff Project, https://www.storyofstuff.org/movies/the-story-of-solutions/(accessed September 13, 2021).

Style, E. (1988) "Curriculum as Window and Mirror," *Listening for all Voices: Gender Balancing the School Curriculum*, 6–12, Summit, NJ: Oak Knoll. Available online: https://nationalseedproject.org/images/documents/Curriculum_As_Window_and_Mirror.pdf (accessed March 30, 2021).

Tannen, D. (1984) *Conversational Style: Analyzing Talk among Friends*, Westport, CT: Ablex.

Trester, A. M. (2017) *Bringing Linguistics to Work: A Story Listening, Story Finding, and Story Telling Approach to Your Career*, Self-published: Lulu.

What Kind of Changemaker Are You?, https://action.storyofstuff.org/survey/changemaker-quiz/(accessed September 13, 2021).

Welcher, L. [Laura Welcher] (June 27, 2019) Language, Meaning, and Culture [Video], YouTube, https://www.youtube.com/watch?v=Y-G6RLhEt10(accessed September 13, 2021).

"Writers of Silicon Valley," https://www.writersofsiliconvalley.com (accessed September 13, 2021).

Wrzesniewski, A., J. M. Berg, and J. E. Dutton (2010) "Managing Yourself: Turn the Job You Have into the Job You Want," *Harvard Business Review*, June. Available online: https://hbr.org/2010/06/managing-yourself-turn-the-job-you-have-into-the-job-you-want# (accessed March 8, 2021).

Index